A CANDLE IN THE WINDOW

A History
of the
Barony of Castleknock

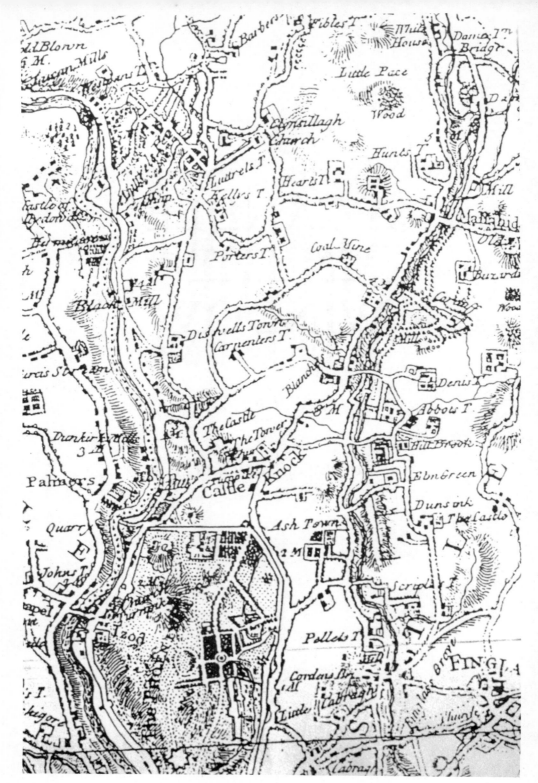

Rocque's map, 1762

A CANDLE IN THE WINDOW

*A History
of the
Barony of Castleknock*

Jim Lacey

MERCIER PRESS

WHAT YOU NEED TO READ

MERCIER PRESS
Douglas Village, Cork
www.mercierpress.ie

Trade enquiries to Columba Mercier Distribution,
55a Spruce Avenue, Stillorgan Industrial Park, Blackrock, Co. Dublin

ISBN: 978 1 85635 552 0

10 9 8 7 6 5 4 3 2 1

Mercier Press receives financial assistance from
the Arts Council/An Chomhairle Ealaíon

Printed in Ireland by ColourBooks

Contents

Drawing of Castleknock Castle circa 1698
Possibly a drawing of Francis Place's original for St Vincent's College,
Centenary Record 1935

Acknowledgements

I wish to acknowledge the enormous assistance I have received from Fr Eugene Kennedy at whose urging I first committed pen to paper in this endeavour. Reverend Pat McGarvey helped me out with proof reading and eased my bafflement with computer technology as did Barry Kilcline who resurrected my computer on several occasions and guided me through its intricacies. Gerry Tynan of The Document Shop was of major assistance in producing the images of prints, photographs and paintings for publishing in disc format, and Alan Halford of Castleknock Lions Club who helped in so many ways.

Local knowledge was gleaned from, among others, the late Fr Doyle C.M. of Castleknock College who gave me a copy of the Centenary Year Book of the college, an invaluable document. Patty Madden, a native of Carpenterstown whose family farmed the land for generations. Mick Harford, Bandmaster, Blanchardstown Band. Katie Bracken from Sandpit Cottages and sister of the late Tommy Bracken local poet and bard. Tom Mongey from Castleknock, Renee Farrell also from Castleknock, the late David Manley whose family were landowners in the area, Paddy O'Leary Blanchardstown, Noel Murray Castleknock, whose local knowledge is second to none Paddy Delaney Annfield, for permission to use the photograph of Archbishop Troy's birthplace, the late Jack Lovely Strawberry Beds, Nora Comiskey Strawberry Beds, Mary Cummins Coolmine and the late Elizabeth Farnan and Phyllis Paterson who first told me of Judge Wylie's connection with Clonsilla. Paul Monahan for all the information on the famous horses trained and bred at Somerton and Abbey Lodge by the Laidlaws. Richie Farrell formerly of Blanchardstown Library and Fingal County Council who gave me access to Library and Archives for the original book. To the courteous and helpful staff of Blanchardstown Library I am also thankful. The Gilbert Library and their staff also gave invaluable assistance. To David Kingston former Managing Director of Irish Life Assurance Plc., I am thankful for his very generous assistance with research expenses for the original edition. To all those whom I can't remember who came to me and said you forgot to put in … or did you know … thanks for the information I hope this edition includes your information.

Finally, I want to thank my wife Geraldine for her constant assistance, in essence she is the co-author of the book.

A Candle in the Window
Painting by Fr Eugene Kennedy

Foreword

The historian Richard Stanihurst (1546–1618) writes of the Castle of Castleknock as follows:

> There is in Castleknock a village not far from Dublin, a window not glazed nor latticed but open, and let the weather be stormy, the wind bluster boisterously on every side of the house and yet place a candle there and it will burn as quietly as if no puff of wind blew; this may be tried at this day, who so shall be willing to put it in practice.

The ruins of Tyrell's castle still incorporate the window; however, the story may relate to the figurative welcoming candle lighting the way for the homecomer. It is interesting to note that during her tenure of office President Mary Robinson drew on the same candle-in-the-window theme as a sign to all our exiles of the welcome home. Áras an Uachtaráin is about two kilometres from Stanihurst's window. Therefore in a special way I similarly dedicate this book to our exiles near and far and hope that it will bring back nostalgic memories.

In order to assist those researching family trees, this new edition has names and addresses of many former residents in alphabetical order in various listings that go back one hundred and fifty years or more.

In keeping with the candle theme. Rathbornes, the oldest candle manufacturers in the world, had associations in this area for nearly 300 years. During a debate in 1985 as to the merits of electric candles as opposed to wax ones, a spokesman for Rathbornes was quoted as saying:

> Rathborne candles incorporate temporal insurance cover in addition to their spiritual attributes when blessed and burned.

As they manufactured candles in Dublin since the early 1400s, perhaps it was one of these which lit the window in Tyrell's castle on the hill of Castleknock.

1

CASTLEKNOCK

OUT OF THE MIST: EARLIEST RECORDS OF CASTLEKNOCK

Castleknock, Cnucha, Duma Meic Eremon, Castrocnok, Thwothyn and Thwetdrom are names that were given to the barony over the ages. Up to the 1960s, the area was almost entirely rural. In the early 1900s F.E. Ball, in his history of County Dublin, wrote of the area that:

> … its southern lands border on a picturesque reach of the River Liffey and its northern lands are intersected by the Tolka, which attains in its passage a high degree of beauty.

William Wordsworth, who visited the area in 1829, said that Castleknock 'possesses a melancholy as well as a wildness peculiarly striking.'

According to lore, the first visitors were the Firbolgs – a race of Celtic origin who came from Greece. Firbolg means 'bagmen,' and these people appeared to have been treated as slaves in Greece; their task was to carry bags of good soil uphill, thus increasing soil fertility on the higher slopes to enable grapes to be grown there. The Firbolg escaped en masse and departed for Ireland.

Cnucha was the wife of Genam or Ruadraidhe and Etar was the wife of Gann. Both Genam or Ruadraidhe and Gann were sons of Dela, a chieftain of the Firbolgs who, with three other sons arrived here 1,000 or more years BC. 'Cnucha died here and Etar died on Benn Etar (Howth Hill) at the same hour.'

In a later saga Cnucha, 'was from the land of Limerick broad and green and she had a beautiful countenance.' She died of an illness, however, and was buried in the centre of a hill. 'Cnucha was then the name given to the hill until the day of judgement.' Previously, this hill, which was called 'Druid's Mound', had been known as a place of pagan rites and used for Druidic ceremonies.

Elim, son of Conn, is mentioned as the valiant king of Cnucha, and his reign was followed by that of Tuathal the Legitimate (one can only speculate as to what the other Tuathal's sobriquet was) and Feidlimid of the Laws, whose son was Conn of the Hundred Battles. Indeed at the time Cnucha was described as a royal dwelling: 'There was not a finer abode save Tara alone.'

Conn supported Criomhtan of the Yellow Hair as king of Leinster, and Cumhal father of Fionn MacCumhail, wanted the throne for Eoghan Mór, king of South Leinster. A great battle occurred, with the Leinster Fianna supporting Cumhal, and the Connacht Fianna, under Aedh Mac Morna, contesting Conn's right. Aedh, who lost an eye and was thereafter known as Goll Mac Morna, killed Cumhal in combat:

> It was by him fell Cumhal the Great
> In the Battle of Cnucha of embattled hosts;
> What they fought this battle for
> Was the Fian Leadership of Fail.

Cumhal was, according to legend, buried in the Tower Hill – also called Windmill Hill – beside Cnucha. Tradition held that the hill was man-made and that the soil for it had been transported in leather bags – in the same way as the Firbolgs were said to carry soil.

The next we hear of Castleknock is a legend relating to a visit by St Patrick to the area, where he called on a prince named Morriahtac – Morinus in some versions – who lived in Cnucha. St Patrick started to preach a sermon to the prince advising him to mend his ways. This topic appeared to hold no interest for Morinus and his head started to nod, his eyes glazed over and shortly afterwards his snoring informed the saint that his words were for nought. Demonstrating that he did not have the patience normally ascribed to saints, Patrick cursed him to sleep until the day of judgement. All that could be done was to build the chambered cnoc over him, and there he sits to this day.

A Mr Quinn, who owned the land before Castleknock College acquired it, had the site investigated by his workmen, who are reputed to have discovered a flight of steps going down into the mound. Whatever they saw when they descended they were struck with fear and dropped their picks and shovels and fled, and none would discuss it afterwards. In the 1880s, the college authorities explored this chamber to a depth of eighty feet until they found a passage to the left and decided to go no further. Various stories tell of a tunnel down to the Liffey or to Knockmaroon Hill ('the Hill of the Secret'). The more likely explanation is that this is an ancient well that was sunk very deep – an essential feature of any castle in case of siege. The well is now a tomb, and the remains of Fr Ferris, one of the college founders, are interred there.

THE NORSE PERIOD

In the year 726 there is a reference to the death of Congalach of Cnucha, but after that there is nothing else mentioned about the area until the battle with the Norsemen and Niall Glún Dubh ('Black Knee'), the ardrí, at Kilmainham on 17 October 919. Niall, who had his house at Castleknock, was killed during this battle. The seventeenth-century *Annals of the Four Masters* contain the following verses in mourning for the fallen leader.

> Where is the Chief of the western world?
> Where the son of every clash of arms?
> The place of great Niall of Cnucha
> Has been changed, ye great wretches.

From this time on there appears to have been some assimilation of the Norsemen, or Vikings, in the Dublin area due to trade and intermarriage. According to local lore, the Norse built a fortress on the hill at that time and there is a tradition that many Welsh settlers found a home in Castleknock during this period.

It is worthwhile to consider the impact Norsemen had on the area. They came first as raiders and plunderers but then gradually settled down and intermarried with the native Irish. They built and developed Dublin as a major port and created a thriving trade between Dublin and the rest of Europe.

There is no evidence that they wore helmets with horns or wings, as they are often represented as having done: this is the product of a nineteenth-century artist's imagination. They settled on the Poddle river near Ship Street (originally Sheep Street) at the south end of Dublin Castle; their settlement extended down to the Wood Quay-High Street area. The Poddle River was important as a source of fresh water, as the Liffey holds brackish salt water as far up as the present-day Heuston Bridge.

THE ENVIRONMENT IN MEDIEVAL DUBLIN

The city would have been incredibly filthy. The streets were cleaned by nature's scavengers – pigs and dogs that roamed wild. Plague occurred in about 1050 and again in 1095. Food poisoning was frequent, owing to contamination and the practice of eating rotten meat. St Anthony's Fire (ergotism), a sometimes-fatal disease caused by rye bread ergot poisoning, was prevalent. In recent years, the nature of this ergot poisoning has been associated with compounds that are used in hallucinatory drugs like LSD.

The ordinary person's diet consisted of milk, curds, cheese and butter. The drinking water would have been unreliable; the Norsemen, like Dubliners to-day, put more store in beer and ale as a thirst-quencher, often knocking back eight pints daily. Stout and porter, however, were unknown at the time – they did not come to Ireland for another 700 or 800 years.

The Norsemen's meat would have been preserved in salt and was quite often so rotten that ginger, pepper, cloves and cinnamon would be used to disguise its taste. The meats and vegetables would have been placed on a flat piece of stale bread shaped like a plate and eaten off this; then the 'plate' itself was eaten or given to the poor. This bread plate, which was called a trencher, was probably the basis for the Italian pizza.

The trencher must have been a great boon to the medieval housewife – it meant that there were no plates and no washing up. The cutlery, if any was used at all, would have been knives; forks are a much later invention. The Irish and Norse women of Dublin could divorce, own and inherit property, claim maintenance and vote at public meetings. In stark contrast, the Anglo-Nor-mans were early male chauvinists who treated their womenfolk with contempt. It was not uncommon then, as in some backward areas of Europe today, for a woman who had prepared a meal to offer it to her husband first and, in his absence, to a male child, or failing that to any male animal before consuming any food herself. Given the earlier mention of food poisoning, however, maybe the womenfolk knew what they were doing.

Most people ate early in the morning and again at night. They killed pigs, and preserved them in salt in early winter. The cattle, which were dry stock, would have been kept outside the town, and the wealthier inhabitants would have eaten beef regularly. The native Irish were known to bleed cattle and mix the blood with herbs and breadcrumbs to produce something like today's black pudding.

Hares were also in great demand. Rabbits were unknown: the Normans introduced them to Ireland. Mutton was not a regular food, the sheep being of more value for their wool. There was a varied seafood diet. The most popular item of seafood was herring, followed by oysters, mackerel, salmon, trout and, of course cockles and mussels. The people of the time bred a small tough breed of hen for poultry and ate wild geese, snipe, woodcock, larks and pigeons.

Their favourite vegetables were onions and leeks. They also cultivated peas and beans, but these were mainly used as fodder for horses – and as food for poorer people. The usual fruits were wild strawberries, blackberries, rowan berries, apples, sloes, cherries, plums and hazelnuts. Coarse wholemeal bread was made from wild grains, barley and rye. The diet our Castleknock ancestors enjoyed was not unlike that of the city folk, with the exception of seafood. The huge Scaldwood of Blanchardstown and Salcocks Wood in Cabra would, apart from berries and nuts, have provided wild boar, which supplemented the meat diet. The potato, which had originated in South America, had not yet been introduced.

In 1938, an exhumation of human remains in an ancient cemetery near the cottages at River Road, Castleknock, revealed some interesting evidence. In total, 380 skeletons, including women and children were exhumed. It was determined that the people practiced Christianity and lived between the ninth and eleventh century. The worn condition of the skeletons' molar teeth showed that the bread eaten was quern-ground and very rough in texture. The remains were those of small, broad-shouldered people with light limbs and broad, short feet. The deltoid muscles of the shoulders developed in such a way that Professor McLoughlin, who supervised the work, concluded that the people used slingshots for hunting and warfare. The site is now an un-marked field and is largely unknown by locals. Its close proximity to Caeveen cemetery, which is discussed later, could indicate that it is the site of an old Christian settlement.

THE NORSE DECLINE

In 1014 Brian Boru, the first Ardrí to secure almost universal acceptance, marched on the Norsemen of Dublin and their Leinster allies and gained victory in a hard-fought battle in which Irish fought Irish and Norse fought Norse. Brian, however who was seventy-three at that time, was in his royal tent – sited, as legend has it, in the middle of what is now Mountjoy Square – where he was slain by the retreating Brodar, one of the Norse leaders. The Irish, un-der Brian had encamped at Kilmainham before the battle, which ranged far and wide from Marino, along the banks of the Tolka River and into Clontarf and Ballybough. Peace reigned in Castleknock from this effective defeat of the Leinstermen until the coming of the Anglo-Normans.

The first bishop of the Dublin Diocese, Dunan (1028–74), was followed by Gille Pádraig, Donngus, and then Samuel Ó Haingli, who died in 1120. There-after, the title archbishop applied, with Gregory officiating from 1152 to 1162, followed by the great St Laurence O'Toole, who governed the see of Dublin during the period of the Anglo-Norman invasions (1162–80). These bishops exercised huge temporal power, ran their own courts, and had their own gaols, palaces and even gallows. The green at Harold's Cross, opposite Mount Jerome Cemetery, was the official place of execution. The reigning bishop was entitled to style himself a baron, and did so. The last Roman Catholic archbishop to employ the baronial device on his coat of arms was Dr John Thomas Troy (1739–1823), a native of Porterstown, Castleknock.

THE NORMANS ARRIVE

In May 1169, the first group of Norman adventurers landed at Bannow Bay and captured Wexford, then a Norse town. Others who landed at the cove of Baginbun reinforced them. Richard Fitzgibbon de Clare (better known as Strongbow), leading the rest of this army, captured Waterford. Dermot Mc-Murrough who, by all accounts, was as fond of the acquisition of wives as he was of the acquisition of land, had invited the Normans to Ireland. He preferred other people's wives; he abducted Dervorgilla, wife of O'Rourke of Breffni. It is conjectured that the Normans would probably have come here without having been invited and Dervorgilla would probably have left O'Rourke without having been abducted.

The Romans who invaded Britain had no interest in Ireland, giving it the name 'Hibernia' from the resemblance of their word for its inhabitants, 'Iverni' to the Latin word for 'wintry'. By contrast, the Normans had considered Ireland as a worthwhile conquest for some time; in 1155 Henry II, who held England and a large portion of France, had secured a papal bull Laudabiliter authorising him to 'proclaim the truths of Christian religion to a rude and ignorant people in Ireland.' The Irish church had had a history of deviance from Roman liturgical practice in some details and up to the time of the reforms of St Malachy was largely a monastic church.

It is perhaps not coincidental that the author of the bull, Adrian IV, was a native of St Albans in Hertfordshire. In any event, the groundwork had been prepared for the invasion beforehand. Whether the bull was authentic or not is still a matter of some debate. It should, however, be noted that Henry II agreed to submit a tax of one penny per house to Rome and that, within 100 years of the invasion, half the land in County Dublin was vested in the church.

On 21 September 1170, Dublin fell to the Normans. Hasculf, the Norse earl of Dublin, made a determined counterattack but this failed and he was beheaded. Meanwhile, Strongbow had assumed the title king of Leinster, having inherited it from his father-in-law Dermot McMurrogh, who had since died. Strongbow married McMurrogh's daughter Aoife immediately after the sack

of Waterford. Rory O'Connor king of Connacht and the last ardrí of Ireland
was eventually stirred into action; he assembled a large army and marched on
Dublin.

THE ROUT AT CASTLEKNOCK

Rory encamped at Castleknock and laid siege to Dublin. His forces numbered
almost 60,000 men according to some sources and stretched from Finglas to
Knockmaroon. It was a huge army that Rory had amassed but 60,000 is perhaps a rather high estimate, given the population of the country and the disu-
nity among the native Irish. The Ulstermen, led by their chieftains O'Rourke
and O'Carroll under MacDunlevy, covered the seashore from Clontarf inland
to Finglas. The army of Hy Kinsella under Murrogh McMurrogh joined up
with the men of Leinster to complete the encirclement on the south side of
Dublin. A fleet of thirty ships of Rory's Norse allies lay at anchor in Dublin
Bay to prevent relief by sea.

The siege, which lasted throughout the summer of 1171, left the Normans
in great difficulty. Their desperation and hunger led them to seek terms. Maurice de Prendergast, with Laurence O'Toole acting as mediator, met with Rory.
An army laying siege to a city, can often become lax and undisciplined due to
inactivity, and that is what happened in this instance. The camp at Castleknock
was the scene of feasting and merriment. De Prendergast shrewdly noted this
and reported back to Strongbow. At Strongbow's command, under cover of
darkness, Miles De Cogan led his knights through Finglas and the remainder
of his force came up directly from Stoneybatter.

The Normans struck at dawn. Rory's forces were completely taken by sur-
prise; Rory himself, who was taking a bath at the time in the Liffey near Glenmaroon had to flee in a state of royal nudity.

Later that year Henry II arrived in Dublin and accepted Strongbow as king
of Leinster. However, he brought with him Hugh de Lacy and gave him the
old fifth province of Meath to act as a counter balance to Strongbow.

HUGH TYRELL GRANTED CASTLEKNOCK

De Lacy granted the 12,001 acres of Castleknock to his man Hugh Tyrell. This area embraced what is now Phoenix Park, Kilmainham, Chapelizod, Clonsilla, Mulhuddart and Castleknock. Copies of the Charters of Hugh de Lacy and Henry II granting Castleknock to Tyrell were discovered in the London Public Records Office in 1933 by Eric St John Brooks. These copies of the originals date back to 1293 and are entirely in Latin – the language for most legal documents at that time. (It is worth remarking that Dublin city would have been Gaelic – and Norse – speaking, with Old English and Norman French also spoken).

The natives of Castleknock would have spoken Gaelic, with the foreigners using Norman French or Old English. In modern English, most words relating to manual or domestic items and functions have Anglo-Saxon roots, while those to do with administration or learning have French roots. This harks back to the time when the 'doers' were the defeated Anglo-Saxons, managed by their Norman French overlords.

The grant is translated thus:

> Henry, by the grace of God, king of England, Lord of Ireland, Duke of Aquitaine and Normandy and Count of Anjou to the Archbishops, Bishops, Ministers and all Earls, Barons, Justices, Sheriffs, Ministers and all his faithful French, English and Irish, greeting. Know that I have conceded, given, and by present Charter confirmed to Hugh Tirel, the man of Hugh de Lacy, Thwothyn and Thwothrom.

The witnesses to the documents are mostly high-ranking Norman noblemen and clergy and include one Stephen Pilat, who gave his name to the townland of Pelletstown near Ashtown. Adam de Feipo is associated with Pilat and de Lacy in other documents. The name Phibsborough is derived from him.

The names Thwothyn and Thwothrom for Castleknock seem to be an attempt to represent the Irish word tuath ('territory'). There is only one other record of the use of either name, in the writ for the inheritance of the estate following the death of the last baron of Castleknock in 1408. Thwothrom may derive from the Irish 'tuath droma', meaning the area of the ridge or a hill ('droim' in Irish).

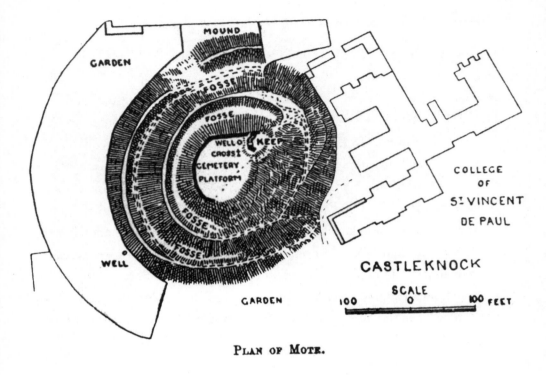

PLAN OF MOTE.

Plan of the mound and ruins at Castleknock from article by M.C. Dix, Irish Builder, *1898*

It is fairly certain from a study of the witnesses' whereabouts during that period – undertaken by Eric St John Brooks in preparing a paper for the Royal Society of Antiquaries in Ireland dated 23 September 1933 – that this grant to Tyrell was drawn up in May 1177. Brooks followed this in 1946 with a paper tracing the ancestry of the Tyrells from Hugh Tyrell, first baron of Castleknock, the son of Rocelin Tyrell of Little Marcle, Herefordshire, and Crowle Siward, Worcestershire. Rocelin Tyrell was in turn descended from Odo Tyrell, who is mentioned as the owner of the same property in the Doomsday Book of 1086.

William the Conqueror, who invaded England in 1066 and defeated Harold at the Battle of Hastings had three sons and one daughter. The eldest son, Robert became duke of Normandy; the second became king of England as William II in 1087. William Rufus as he was known, was mysteriously shot by an arrow while hunting in the New Forest in Hampshire. A Walter Tyrell appears to have fired the arrow that, accidentally or otherwise, ended his reign.

William Rufus' brother Henry I, the third son of the Conqueror, then inherited the throne. His death – from overeating – was followed by a bitter civil war between his daughter Matilda and a nephew Stephen that lasted until Stephen's death, after which Henry II restored civic order. So it was that Henry II granted Castleknock to a descendant of the man whose arrow killed his great-uncle and changed the royal succession. Hugh de Lacy also charged Tyrell with the wardenship of Trim Castle, the largest castle in Ireland. This castle was sacked by Rory O'Connor, however, and Tyrell had to retrieve it with the help of Raymond Fitzgerald.

THE EIGHT BARONS

Eight barons of Castleknock occupied the castle for the next 200 years. Hugh was succeeded by Richard, who was succeeded by Hugh, who was succeeded by Richard, and so on until 1364. Richard, the fourth baron acceded in or about 1270. Hugh the fifth baron took over in 1295. He died in 1299, to be followed by the sixth baron, who died during Christmas 1321 and whose son Hugh inherited the title of seventh baron in 1364 despite the fact that he was still a minor. Hugh's son Robert died in 1370, along with his wife Scholastica and his son and heir, from the black plague which was sweeping Europe at the time. Robert was the eighth and last Baron of Castleknock. Thus ended the Tyrell dynasty; the castle and lands passed to Robert's two sisters. Before discussing the next owners of Castleknock, we can look at some of the exploits of these Tyrells.

Hugh Tyrell, the first baron, had a falling-out with Hugh de Lacy and shifted allegiance to Philip de Worcester, who had supplanted de Lacy as justiciar (chief justice and the supreme power in Norman Ireland) by supporting him in a campaign against the Irish. It is said that the Normans seized from the monks in Armagh a large cauldron or brewing pan, among other things. The monks cast maledictions and curses on the plunderers' heads, with the curious result that everything with which the cauldron came in contact ignited. The stolen goods were returned with great speed.

The first baron, in contrast, went on the third crusade and participated in the Siege of Acre. He bestowed lands on the priory of John the Baptist at Kilmainham and brought the Benedictine monks from Little Malvern in Worcestershire to found a monastery – the Abbey of St Brigid in Castleknock. The fact that these monks originated in Worcestershire could indicate a political move by Tyrell to gain favour with the justiciar. Tyrell died in 1199 and was buried in Selincourt.

His third son, Richard, succeeded the first baron. The eldest son, Walter, was given Poix in France, the second son received land in Hampshire, and Roger, another son, held land in Tipperary and was the king's bailiff for Co. Louth.

According to *Balls History of County Dublin*, this period brought uninterrupted prosperity to Castleknock, which was known as the 'Land of Peace.' The second baron, Richard Tyrell, fought alongside Richard the Lion-Heart at Dieppe when Philip II of France tried to seize the English king's French possessions.

Richard Tyrell was known as the Red Baron. He fell into disfavour with King John and Henry III, John's son. This may have been because of power struggles between Walter de Lacy and the king; due to his association with the de Lacys, Tyrell would have been involved in these conflicts. John was a strong, ruthless individual of whom the chroniclers of the day, like many people since, had a poor opinion:

> John, nature's enemy. He plundered his own. Cruel towards all men. Hell itself is fouled by the presence of John. No man may ever trust him.

He was finally forced by the English barons to sign the Magna Carta at Runnymede in 1215.

Although the Tyrells' struggle with the king may have been associated with his conflict with the English barons, resistance to the punitive taxes imposed by John to fund some of his many wars may also have been a significant factor in the Tyrells' opposition to him. At any rate, the castle was forfeited to the crown during this period but was returned on receipt of an undertaking as to future conduct. It is possible that a son was taken hostage to ensure the promise was kept.

In 1214, the castle was ordered to be demolished. As this did not happen, in 1218 the command was issued again, in the name of Henry III, who was then only eleven years old. It was only because of the practice of hostage-taking that the castle was saved; the castle was saved again in similar circumstances in 1221.

The third baron, Hugh, enjoyed better relations with his king and attended him at his court in France. He became king's seneschal in Ireland and married the daughter of Justiciar Geoffrey de Marisco. He also served with the king in Gascony against the king of Castille.

Hugh is mentioned in a royal deed as having the right to hold a fair at Newtown Fertuallagh, County Westmeath, another vast holding, which the family owned.

The fourth baron, Richard, has a record of royal service on a military expedition to Roscommon. The fifth baron, Hugh, is mentioned as the one on whose instruction the copy of the grant quoted previously was drawn up. This copy was possibly used in a dispute which the fifth baron had with Stephen de Fulburn, justiciar and treasurer, in respect of feudal dues owed. At this time the following families had settled in the area: Abbots in Abbotstown, de la Felde in Corduff, Pilates in Pelletstown and Blanchards from Tipperary, who were connected to the Tyrells in Blanchardstown. (The Blanchards' name comes from 'blanchet', meaning 'white'; the name Plunkett may have the same origin).

The Keppoks, from County Louth, who were connected with the Carpenters of Carpenterstown, settled in Cappagh. Sheriff Woodlock, of Dublin lived near the castle, as did the Serjeants family, who later intermarried with the Tyrells. The Luttrells of Luttrellstown appear around this period as landowners and later assumed most of the power in the area. The Deuswells settled in Diswellstown, as did the Kerdiff family in Cardiffsbridge. The sixth baron, Richard, served under Edward I (1239–1307), known as Longshanks, in his invasion of Scotland, when he removed the Stone of Scone to Westminster and overthrew the Scottish monarchy.

During this period, the O'Byrnes and O'Tooles, raiding from the fastness of the Wicklow Mountains, caused some of those living south of the river to move to the 'Land of Peace'. One Paul Lagheles, however, had 200 sheep stolen from him by Louth men who were coming to lend support against the mountain men. There was an offer of trial by combat, which Lagheles did not accept, and he ended up in prison.

This Richard had an interesting dispute with the lord chief justice – which no doubt he lost. An eagle frightened a valuable falcon owned by the lord chief justice while it was being bathed in the river at what is now College Green; the startled bird arrived in Castleknock, where Richard detained it. Richard was apparently aware that it had been announced missing. A twenty-shilling reward was offered for the bird, and the case went to court, with the chief justice seeking £20 damages. The falcon was handed over and proceedings were dropped.

Richard had a younger brother called John, who seems to have been something of a scoundrel. There was bad blood between him and John Deuswell, a tenant of the baron, who lived in Deuswellstown (Diswellstown). In 1305 Richard's brother John struck a servant of the Deuswells and attempted to attack John and Hugh Deuswell but was chased off when John Deuswell drew a dagger to defend himself. Richard's brother returned later, armed and on horseback, and attacked again with stones. Eventually he was gaoled for assault and trespass. Later John was in trouble for stealing food belonging to 'divers poor men' and selling it. When charged, he escaped, threatening a bailiff with an axe. Having been re-arrested, he had to give his horse as a gage for the debt he incurred and was again gaoled. He is the most likely culprit in the legend of the White Lady of Castleknock, which is discussed later.

In the year 1316 Edward Bruce, brother of Robert, king of Scotland, having been crowned at Faughart near Dundalk, marched on Dublin. He arrived at Castleknock on the feast of St Matthew, 21 September, at the head of 20,000 soldiers, captured the castle and held the Baron Richard and his wife until a ransom was paid. The fortifications in Dublin proved too strong for Bruce to attack successfully and he retreated towards Leixlip and returned to Faughart, where he was killed in battle in October 1318. The city walls beside St Audeon's Arch were rebuilt and strengthened that week and a fragment of these walls, with steps and arched gateway, still remains. Richard died during Christmas 1321 after a very eventful life and was succeeded by his son Hugh, who was almost twenty-one at the time and had an unremarkable tenure until he died in 1364.

The eighth and last baron lived for only six years after inheriting the title. He died with his wife and child in 1370 from the bubonic plague, then ravaging all Europe. This plague, or Black Death as later historians called it, was carried by fleas from black rats to humans. The cause of the plague was not known for hundreds of years after and was one of the greatest disasters to strike humankind.

The plague symptoms were large swellings, or buboes (hence the name 'bubonic' plague), some as large as tennis balls, under the armpits and groin. Black and blue blotches all over the body followed these. The victim's breath turned rancid, and blood was vomited. Most died within three days of being infected with the disease. The unsanitary conditions in which people lived and the almost complete inattention to hygiene contributed to the spread of this and many other diseases. In fact the current thinking is that it may have been a separate virus altogether that occurred alongside bubonic plague.

The severity of the plague in Dublin city was such that mass graves or pits were dug on the outskirts of the city for the victims. To this day the area is known as Blackpits.

CHANGING TIMES

The only survivors of the plague entitled to the Castleknock estate were Joan and Matilda – sisters of the baron – who both married twice and for whom the estate was divided. Joan's second husband, William Boltham, held the castle until 1408, when he died and his stepson Thomas Serjeant, son of Joan's first husband, got possession of it. The details of the writ describe the estate as consisting of the castle of Castleknock with six messuages and two carucates (a season's ploughing of a team of oxen) of arable land, meadow and pasture and seven acres of wood, one messuage and half a carucate of land in Irishtown (now known as the Fifteen

Acres, in fact it consists of nearly 300 acres), six messuages and a carucate and a half of land in Thwothyn – all valued at ten marks.

The tenants are listed as John Owen in Blanchardstown and Diswellstown; Richard Plunkett in Astagob; William Porter in Barberstown and Fynnagh-land Porterstown; Robert Luttrell in Timolin; the prioress of Lismullen near Tara having Kellystown, the Grange of Clonsilla and the White Chapel of St Macolthus (Mochta) at Coolmine under the prior of Malvern; James Reynolds in Clonsilla; Walter Rendvell in Renvelstown; Christopher Plunkett in the Pass; Gerald Tyrell in Powerstown; Henry Scurlagh in Kilmartyn; William Cruise in Cruiserath; and the prior of St John's outside Newgate, Ashtown. This last parcel included some of the present Phoenix Park.

This list of tenants includes names of families associated with the area up to relatively recent times. The *Dublin Evening Mail* for 18 March 1825 carried the following obituary:

> Died at Sandymount 13th. ult. Elizabeth, youngest daughter of Henry Porter esq., formerly of Porterstown in the County of Dublin.

This appeared to be the last of the family line of the Porters of Porterstown. The Castleknock estate devolved on Thomas Serjeant but it remained with him only fleetingly, as he died within the year; his son John took possession of it.

THE BURNELL ERA

The estate remained in the family until Chief Justice Sir Nicholas Barnewell secured it through intermarriage. It then passed to Roland Eustace, baron of Portlester, and later to the Burnell family. The Burnell interest arose through John Burnell, the second husband of Matilda. Burnell's chief seat was Balgriffin and he did not reside in Castleknock as frequently as his predecessors did. He was later attainted for his part in the rebellion of Silken Thomas in 1537. It was during this era that Richard Stanihurst (1547–1618) wrote of the unquenchable candle mentioned in the foreword.

John's son, Henry, was a brilliant lawyer who represented the Irish cause at the Royal Court in London. He acted as counsel for Gerald, eleventh earl of Kildare. His efforts were so zealous that he ended up for a time as a prisoner, in the Tower of London.

John Burnell argued strongly for the repeal of Poynings Law which subjected the Irish to all English laws, and was the main mover in a petition for toleration of the Roman Catholic faith. He was appointed recorder of Dublin in 1573 and justice of the queen's bench in spite of his professed Catholicism. By the time of his death in 1614, a great deal of his power had dissipated because of the fact that he had offended the establishment too often. He was buried in the parish church of St Brigid, where an aisle was dedicated as the Burnell Chapel. Philip Hoare and Christopher Barnewell subsequently became the occupants, following Burnell's son and grandson.

THE CONFEDERATION WARS

In the 1641 rebellion the castle was secured for the Irish forces under Owen Roe O'Neill. Lieutenant Thomas Bringhurst was given seventy musketeers, two sergeants, and three corporals to capture the castle but failed to do so. General Monk, later the duke of Albermarle, diverted his march to Athlone to attack the castle. Eighty people were killed in the unsuccessful defence of the castle, and other defenders were hanged. In 1647, Owen Roe retook the castle; he did not stay there, however, but instead laid waste to a large part of the county. These various onslaughts on the castle caused such damage that from this date the structure seriously deteriorated.

THE WHITE LADY OF CASTLEKNOCK

Roger Tyrell is the villain of the legend of the White Lady of Castleknock, which is set in the sixteenth century and is related in Burton's History of the Royal Hospital of Kilmainham. If it has any historical basis, the story should have occurred 200 years earlier, and the villain of the piece would have been one John Tyrell, brother of the sixth baron, Richard. John Tyrell's *curriculum vitae* would admirably suit the story.

One of the Wicklow chieftains O'Byrne settled in Ballyfermot on the hill overlooking Chapelizod. He was blessed with a most beautiful daughter named Eileen. John Tyrell, unknown to his brother the baron, who was abroad at the time, seized the fair Eileen for his own lustful pursuits.

He imprisoned her in a room in the castle. At the dead hour of night, she heard Tyrell's footsteps on the staircase and, rather than submit to him, she bled to death by opening her veins with the large pin of the brooch that fastened her cloak. O'Byrne attacked the castle with great fury and killed John Tyrell. This was not enough to save his beloved daughter, however. From then onwards glimpses of a ghostly apparition are seen to glide mournfully around the ruins of Castleknock Castle.

Another legend says that it is St Brigid who appears every seven years near to the church she founded. This story of St Brigid relates to other sites connected with her and may have a pre-Christian origin. *The Nation* newspaper related the legend in verse:

> When the distant chimes sound midnight hour
> The spirit pure is seen,
> And moving round the lonely tower
> Looks bright as moonlight beam.
> And as the moonbeams tint the walls
> And light the turret's crest
> 'Twas hence she says my spirit fled
> 'Tis here my bones find rest.
> And here I wander year by year
> For such my lot has been,
> But soon at end my penance drear,
> I'll rest in joy unseen.

THE CROMWELLIAN WARS AND CIVIL SURVEY

By 1647 Thomas Bringhurst, who had attempted to take Castleknock Castle during the 1641 rebellion and was now Mayor, had come into possession of the castle under the Cromwellian settlement. He held it for only a short time, however. The brief of the Civil Survey (1654–56), which was set up as a preliminary to land confiscations, reads as follows:

> In pursuance of a commission and instructions (amongst others) directed unto us ye right Honble. Lord Deputy and council bearing date the 4th of October 1654. Wee have as well by jury ye most knowing and sufficient men of ye Barony of Castleknock as by all other lawful wages and meanes in our power endeavoured to fine out the landes of ye said Barony with their quality, quantity, value in ye year sixteen hundred and forty etc.

The survey shows 'Christopher Barnewell, an Irish papist' as the proprietor of the castle and lands of 232 acres, of which '10 is in meadow, 180 in arable, 5 in pasture and 37 in shrub wood and ffues. The property is in mortgage to William Warren of Coolduffe (Corduff)'. The buildings on the property are described as 'an old castle together with one thatched house and stable with several other cottages also one orchard'.

In the survey 'Symon Luttrell an Irish papist holds lands in Clonsillagh and ye Grange, Barberstown, Kishandstown, Cunmeneetown, Phelblestown, Barryageyth, Stahenny, part of Blanchardstown, part of Carpenterstown, Ballystrowan, Skirmullin, Kellystown.' Christopher Barnwell 'an Irish papist' has lands in 'Hartstown, Blanchardstown, Irishtown (the fifteen acres in Phoenix Park). 'Matthew Barnwell (has) little Stahenny, Carpenterstown; Sir Edward Bolton an English Protestant (has) Culmine and Ringwellstown.' (This estate was sold to Alexander Kirkpatrick by Robert Bolton in 1782). The city of Dublin 'owened lands at Ballicollan.' 'Philip Hore Irish papist (holds) the Churchtown (this is obviously where the estate divided after the death of the last Tyrell baron) Lr Irishtown.'

The survey continues: 'Henry Segrave Irish papist little Cabragh (the Segraves remained in the Cabra area until the early 1900's). 'Robert Dil-

EXTRACT FROM DOWN SURVEY

244   BARONY OF CASTLEKNOCK

Syr̃h Luttrell Aforesayd.	Diswellstown	Two hundred & Twelve Acres.	Mead, 12 Arab: 160 Pastur: 40		By the Jury Ninty four pound. By us One hundred & six pounds.

OBSERVATIONS.

To the Proprietor. The Proprietor held the premisses Anno: 1641 as his Inheretance.

Buildings. Theire is upon the premisses one stone house with other houses of Office & severall smale Cottages valleved by the Jury at One hundred pounds.

Tythes. The Tythes belonge to St Robt Meredith.

Boundes. Bounded on the East with the lands of Castleknock on the South with the River Liffy on the West the Land of Stagobb on the north wth Culmine.

36   PARISH OF CASTLE KNOCK.

Proprietors Names, &c.	Denominačon of Lands	Number of Acres	Profitable Lands	Unprofitable Lands	Vallew Annó: 1640
Geo: Hackett of Stagobb Ir: Papist.	Stagob ½ a Plowland.	Eighty Acres.	Mead: 01 Arab: 60 Pastũ 16	Shrubby Wood } 03	By the Jury Twenty pounds By Us Thirty five pounds.

OBSERVATIONS

To the Proprietor. The proprietor helde the premisses Anno: 1641 as his Inheretanc.

Tythes. The Tythes Belonged to the rectory of Clonsillagh.

Boundes. Bounded on the East with Diswellstowne on the South with the Liffy on the west the Lands of Luttrellstowne on the north with Porterstowne.

Edw: Dowde of Porterstown Ir: Papist.	Porterstow ½ a Plo: land.	One hundred Acres.	Mead: 06 Arable 80 Pastur 14		By the Jury Twenty eight pounds. By Us fifty pounds.

OBSERVATIONS.

To the Proprietor. The Proprietor held the premisses Anno: 1641 as his Inheritance.

Buildings. Theire is upon the premisses one small Castle and two or three Cottages valleved by the Jury at sixty pounds One Orchard & Garden & severall Ash trees for Ornamt about ye House.

Tythes. The one moyety of the Tythes Belonge to St Robt Meredith the other to the Rectory of Clonsillagh.

Boundes. Bounded on the East to the Lands of Diswellstown on the South with Stagobb on the West with the Land of Ballystrane on the north the land of Cullmine.

Extract from Down Survey, Sir William Petty 1655

lon Irish papist Blanchardstown (the Dillon family were landowners until recent times). Edward Dowde Irish papist Porterstown. Katherine Stronge Irish papist Danielstown (near Barn Lodge); Sir John Dungan Irish papist – Abbotstown; Lord Dunsany Irish papist – the Ffullams, between Abbotstown and Ballycoolan' (the lords of Dunsany are Plunketts of the family of St Oliver Plunkett and Plunketts are still lords of Dunsany to this day – in all, twenty generations of Plunketts); Lord Fitzwilliam Irish papist – Keppuck' (now Cappagh).

Will 'Warren Irish papist – Corduff' (he also held the castle and its lands in mortgage at this time and his family resided in the area until relatively recent times); 'Mr Agart Protestant – great Cabragh' (mostly lands that later were acquired by the Dominican nuns); 'John Connell protestant – Ashtown' (on whose lands Ashtown Castle, the former papal nunciature, still stands. In fact the remainder still standing is the original castle, the more recent part having succumbed to dry rot. John Connell was an ancestor of the O'Connells of Caherdaniel, of whom Daniel O'Connell the Liberator was a member.

The survey continues: Robert Bysse protestant – Pellistowne; Henry Power Lord of Vallentia protestant – St Laurence Land (within Castleknock parish); Ignatius Mapus protestant – Abbotstown; Lord of Howth protestant – part of the Ffullams; Sir Robert Loftus protestant – Schriblestown, Dunsinck. Barth Dillon protestant – Keppuck; Christ Church – Stagob.'

The foregoing gives a fairly accurate picture of the landholding in the barony at this time. There was also a large mill in Castleknock that was known as the Red Mill and was owned by Roger Sprotton.

THE HEARTH TAX ROLL

A further insight into the occupancy of land at this period is given by the rolls used in connection with the Hearth Money Act, which required all householders to pay a tax for each chimney or hearth in their house. The tax amounted to the not inconsequential sum of two shillings. A fairly accurate indication of the wealth of an individual was the number of chimneys he had. Hence, Thomas

Luttrell, with twelve chimneys at Luttrellstown Castle, would appear to have been the wealthiest, followed by Lord Orrery in Porterstown, with nine and John Warren of Castleknock, with four. (At this time, the power in the area shifts from the occupiers of Castleknock Castle to the Luttrell family). The roll also lists the following:

James Russell of Coolmine
Richard Dempsey, Blanchardstown
Robert Broghill, Clonsilla

A number of householders are listed as having one chimney each; their family names still largely survive in the barony to this day. They include Dunne (later large landowners in Ashtown), Egan, Lawler, Glany, Hickey, Murphy and Murtagh, all of Castleknock; Lock (this family lived in the area until recent times and were connected with the culture of strawberries that gave its name to the Strawberry Beds); Farmer, English and Wood all of Porterstown. In Blanchardstown, we find Dempsey, Boylan, Callaghan, Skully, Jordan, Gargan, Plunkett, Bamber, Lowth, Rourke and Cosgrave. In Carpenterstown there are two families – Quinn and Buggil – and in Clonsilla the following names appear: Devlin, Beaghan, Mallone, Tuite, Moran, Malloy, Murphy, Feeny, Coghan, Keegan, Jordan, Carolan, Ivers, Barry and Boylan. The names Fluddy, Lynch, Kelly, Treacy, Mortimer, Lawless, Deamish and Joy appear for Coolmine.

Castleknock Castle 1698
From a copy of Francis Place's original. Painting by Fr Eugene Kennedy

Castleknock Castle 1791
From a copy of Cocking's drawing in Grose' Antiquities
Painting by Fr Eugene Kennedy

This period was a time of unprecedented religious, social and political up-heaval with land changing hands and families shifting between the Protestant Established church and the Roman Catholic church in order to preserve land and ancient titles. It was an era of lawlessness and bloody strife. Land deterio-rated, crops were destroyed and thousands perished in war.

WOLVES AT LARGE

Such was the devastation in the barony that land became once again untamed and the great Scaldwood of Blanchardstown reclaimed through natural regene-ration those areas on its margin which had succumbed to the plough. The sus-pension of hunting for pleasure led to a dramatic increase in wolves in the area. These wolves were a particular menace to livestock, especially lambs and calves; wolves, being opportunistic hunters, prey mostly on young or sick animals. The threat of wolves to man has always been exaggerated, however. The authorities organised a wolf cull in the year 1652, and this is the last reference to wolves in the area. Within decades, they became extinct in Ireland due to over-hunting.

THE DOWN SURVEY

Dr William Petty, who was physician-in-chief to the Cromwellian army, under-
took the survey of the country in 1654. He employed soldiers, as they were
trained in using the instruments required for mapping and were able and experienced in working under difficult conditions. The survey was called The Down
Survey because the details were set down on maps as well as tables.

The Down Survey maps were so well drawn that they were not bettered until
the Ordnance Survey of 1825-41. The original maps were lost in the destruction
of the Four Courts in 1922 and another copy held in British archives in London
was lost in a fire. The only surviving copy of the period is not only of historical
significance but it is a superb work of art. It was seized by a French man-o'-war
from a British vessel and is now in the Bibliothéque Nationale in Paris.

THE MAJESTIC RUIN

Meanwhile, Castleknock Castle had fallen into a semi-ruinous condition.
Francis Place's drawings of the castle in 1698 show several thatched dwellings
around the base and depict a much more substantial building than that por-
trayed in Cocking's 1791 drawing in Groses Antiquities. Nonetheless, Place's
drawings show the castle being unoccupied and semi-derelict. The condition
of the ruin in 1791 is very similar to what we see today. It is believed that John
Warren sold large quantities of stone from the castle to Luke Gardiner when
he built his residence, which was later to become Mountjoy Barracks, now the
Ordnance Survey Offices in Phoenix Park.

In 1666, the castle and land became the property of a distinguished Norman family, the Warrens of Corduff, latterly of Warrenstown, Co. Meath. This
property included the site of the Ordnance Survey Offices and the Guinness
estates of Farmleigh and Knockmaroon. The Warrens leased from time to time
these lands to different tenants; they eventually became the property of Rev.
William Gwynn, having previously been leased by Rev. David Brickell, who
had it from John Chalmely.

Castleknock College, circa 1854
Courtesy of late Fr Doyle, Castleknock College

Present outlet for St Brigid's Well
Photograph by Fr Eugene Kennedy

Rev. Gwynne and a Mr Andrew Swanzy opened a seminary there for young Protestant gentlemen. This was not, however, a seminary as we understand the word nowadays (an instruction for the education and training of young men for the church); all high-class educational establishments then were called seminaries.

THE COLLEGE

In 1834 Rev. John McCann purchased, on behalf of the Vincentian community of St Vincent's Seminary, 34 Ushers Quay, the lands described as Castlefield, the Windmill field, the Limekiln field, the Hop field. These lands embraced the two hills there and amounted to forty acres. The lands also included a disused lead mine, which was worked in about 1744 for a short period. This mine and its excavations may have given rise to legends about mysterious tunnels and passages. Green spotting indicates that there may also have been some copper present in the stones. In addition, on the property adjoining the Church of Ireland churchyard there was a well described by Grose as 'beneficial to human beings but poisonous to lower animals.' An earlier scribe says it was 'noxious to lower animals but potable to man and the higher beasts.'

This seems to have been the original St Bridget's Well of Castleknock; the well's outlet was moved to the pump opposite the side of Myos public house, where the present inhabitants of the barony consume other potable liquids.

There is a plaque on either side of the pump. On one side is inscribed 'Jesus said whosoever drinketh of the water that I shall give them shall never thirst;' and on the other: 'and he shall lead them into living fountains of water and God shall wipe away all tears from their eyes.'.

The college's founding is connected with that of Maynooth College, in which Archbishop Troy, a native of Porterstown, played a significant part. Before their ordination, four clerical students decided to set up a religious community. They were Peter Kenrick, Anthony Reynolds, Michael Burke and James Lynch, a qualified surgeon then studying for the priesthood. At first they met with opposition, but the Dean of Maynooth College Fr Dowley and Fr Meagher joined with them, along with Fr Scurlog, Fr McNamara and Fr McCann, a lawyer. Together, they formed the Congregation of the Missions, or the Vincentians.

The Vincentians had a long and honoured history in Ireland, providing missions during the Penal days. One young Vincentian, Timothy Lee, had his hands and feet cut off before his mother's eyes by Cromwell's soldiers before being finally put to death at his home near Adare.

Fr Edward Ferris, who is buried at the foot of the castle, was a native of Kerry born in 1738 who served with the Irish Brigade in France. He became a Vincentian and rose to become assistant-general of the Congregation. He had to flee during the French Revolution; wounded and covered in blood, he barely escaped with his life. Dr Troy encouraged him to take up the position of Dean and later

Lt Col. Reynolds, VC, Surgeon at Rorke's Drift Zulu Wars

professor of Maynooth. In 1875, special permission was granted so that his remains could be reinterred with those of his brother Vincentians in Castleknock.

Castleknock College has been noted as a cradle of learning for churchmen, the medical profession, the legal profession and the military. Lt Col Reynolds, VC, the hero of Rorke's Drift (1879) in the Zulu wars, was a past pupil, as was Admiral Sir H.C. Kane, who saved the Calliope in a hurricane in Samoa in 1889. During the First Vatican Council (1869–70) Bishop Moran of Dunedin, New Zealand, Bishop Grimly of Cape of Good Hope, South Africa, Bishop Feehan of Nashville, Tennessee, Bishop Fennelly of Madras, India and Archbishop Lynch of Toronto must have felt a sense of *déjà vu:* they had all been classmates from Castleknock!

Lord Russell of Killowen

Many other prelates also had Castleknock for their alma mater. These included Bishop Gilloly of Elphin, Bishop Kilduff of Ardagh, Bishop Leonard of Cape Town, Bishop Donnelly of Canea, and Bishop Ryan of Philadelphia and Bishop Ryan of Sale, Australia.

Lord Russell of Kilowen, who in 1894 became the first Roman Catholic to hold the position of lord chief justice of England since the Reformation, was a Castleknock pupil. Before this, he was elected as Liberal MP for Dundalk in 1880. He also held the post of attorney general in Gladstone's two Home Rule governments. Russell was leading advocate for Parnell at the Parnell Commission trial. He exposed Richard Piggot the forger. Piggot was asked to write down some words – one of which was the word hesitancy. Piggot spelled the word 'hesitency' – the same way it was spelt in the forged letters. This opened the way for a rigorous cross-examination. Further inconsistencies were revealed, prompting him to flee to Madrid, where he is alleged to have shot himself. Parnell was thus vindicated.

In the sporting arena, Castleknock's feats, particularly in rugby, are well known and Castleknock is still a formidable side. A perusal of staff members shows Éamon de Valera, BA, teaching maths in 1910–11 to pupils in Castleknock. We can only speculate as to what would have transpired had Dev continued in the groves of academia. Liam Cosgrave, who like his godfather Éamon de Valera, also served as Taoiseach, was a student in the college. Another celebrity to grace the lawns of Castleknock, albeit more fleetingly, was Queen Victoria. She visited Castleknock to show her gratitude to the Irish regiments for their loyalty during the Boer War, which was in progress at the time. She arrived on a fine Sunday evening in April and spent some time chatting to the students. The president of the college, Fr Geoghegan, told the queen some of the history relating to the castle; his remarks seemed to interest her greatly.

Miss Mary Emmeline Breen who resigned in 1981 at the ripe old age of 93 having reigned as postmistress of Castleknock for 56 years witnessed the visit. She recalled that as a child of about twelve she was sitting on the wall outside her home at Oak Cottage when the royal coach with entourage trundled down the Castleknock Road. Her majesty was ensconced in the back of the coach 'with all the appearance of a grumpy old lady', as Miss Breen observed at the time.

2

LUTTRELLSTOWN

The Luttrell family occupied the other great power base in the area, Luttrellstown, for nearly 500 years. The first Luttrell connected with Ireland was Sir Geoffrey, a supporter of King John.

There is a rumour that King John stayed at Luttrellstown Castle, and parts of the castle could indeed be that ancient. From Geoffrey descend the Luttrells of Dunster Castle, Somersetshire, who also owned the Isle of Lundy in the British Channel and had estates at Carhampton in Somerset and Irnham in Lincolnshire. The Irish Luttrells were a distinguished family for generations but sadly some members of the family brought the name into disrepute, and the name of Luttrell in the barony is remembered more for the negative influences of these black sheep than for the good associated with their earlier ancestors.

THE EARLY LUTTRELLS

The Luttrells were in the vanguard of William the Conqueror's army at the Battle of Hastings and amassed large estates as a reward for their service to the crown. The name Luttrell appears to come from l'outre, the French word for otter. Geoffrey Luttrell first appeared in Ireland in 1204 as a member of a royal commission appointed by King John with a brief to settle some disputes between the Norman barons possibly related to land. He purchased his estate with twenty ounces of gold. Geoffrey assisted King John on his Irish expedition of 1210 and was later to act as his ambassador to the Pope.

King John had quarrelled with Innocent III over the appointment of the archbishop of Canterbury, and England had been placed under an interdict, with John himself excommunicated. Luttrell never returned to Ireland, as he died on this royal errand. Robert Luttrell became lord chancellor of Ireland in 1236 and held this powerful position for ten years. He was also treasurer of St Patrick's cathedral. There is a record of a Michael Luttrell settling a legal debt in 1287 for John de Kerdiff of Kerdiff's Castle, Finglas; the Kerdiff family name persists today in the name Cardiff Bridge. A Simon Luttrell is mentioned in the old records as having the lease of a salmon weir on the Liffey at St Wolstan's near Lucan.

Robert Luttrell, the chancellor, married into the Plunkett family. This was the start of numerous marriage alliances with wealthy Norman families that resulted in substantial land acquisitions. The Luttrells intermarried with the Bellew, Sarsfield, Travers, Fitz Lyon, Barnewell, Aylmer, Bathe, Dillon, Finglas, Segrave, St Laurence, Fitzwilliam and Goulding families. The culmination of these marriage alliances occurred in 1771, when Anne Luttrell married Henry, duke of Cumberland, brother of King George III. In fact, there was a lot of intermarriage between the lords of the Pale for centuries, and the histories of these families are completely interwoven.

THE LUTTRELLS DURING THE REFORMATION

The Rt Hon. Sir Thomas Luttrell, the sixteenth-century chief justice of Common Pleas, was noted for his grasp of law and his fluency in Gaelic. He also held the position of solicitor general. He remained loyal to the doctrines of Rome while acknowledging the Act of Supremacy, whereby Henry VIII appointed himself supreme governor of the Church of England. Thomas Luttrell's religious mores did not prevent him from sharing in the spoils from the dissolution of monasteries; as he acquired the lands of St Mary's abbey at Coolmine.

Indeed, as chief baron of the exchequer he was actually involved in the dissolution. When he died in 1554, he was enormously wealthy and the church in Clonsilla had to be extended to make room for his tomb. He made provision for this expense in his will and left money for the repair of the chancel and the rebuilding of the bridge over the Tolka at Mulhuddart. Such was the extent of his wealth that the crown borrowed money from his estate.

His son Christopher survived him as heir to Luttrellstown but only lived two years. He was replaced by his brother James, Sheriff of County Dublin, who died in 1557 much to the regret of his tenantry, as he had been a good landlord, treating his tenants well and having a charitable disposition. James Luttrell was married to Genet Sarsfield from Lucan; he was her second husband and she went on to have another three! The couple had a child that died in infancy and the estate went to the third son, Simon, who was a law student but settled down to run the estate. He later assisted in mustering an army against Shane O'Neill. His second wife, Elizabeth Finglas, survived him.

The Finglas family were the original owners of Dunsoghly Castle near St Margaret's, which later became the property of the Plunketts. This castle is in a good state of repair, and the roof was recently refurbished, with some of the original oak timbers being kept intact. Parts of the film *Braveheart* were shot there.

The Luttrell family still retained their Roman Catholic faith but outwardly must have given some recognition to the established church in order to hold their lands. It should be remembered that, although he broke with Rome, Henry VIII kept very much to the traditional religious practices. His son Edward, a sickly youth, controlled to great extent by his ministers, brought in reforms, which were subsequently reversed by Mary and reinstated by Elizabeth. In fact, as a young princess, Elizabeth often attended Mass when politic to do so. The religious leaders of that time were often as fickle: Hugh Curwen, archbishop of Dublin (1557–67) hopped from the Protestant faith to the Catholic one and back again as often as the monarchs changed, and other prelates did the same. This was in contrast to the many churchmen, Catholic and Protestant, who suffered and indeed, often died, for their beliefs.

Simon's eldest son, Thomas, who inherited the estate, was very active in the cause of the Irish Catholics. He was imprisoned twice for his actions on their behalf during the reign of James I. His great wealth and influence gave him a measure of protection, however, and he was allowed into favour. On his death in 1635 he left his wife Alison Diswellstown House, twenty cows, three hundred sheep, six rams, fifteen farm horses, four riding horses and a huge amount of silver plate. To his younger children he left gold and silver coins of immense value, and his eldest son Simon received the castle and demesne.

During this time, Archbishop Bulkely of the established church complained of 'Mass Houses and Popish Schools' in the locality which were sponsored by the Luttrells. Fr Paul Harris from England acted as chaplain to the Luttrell family and said Masses in the area, as did Fr Patrick Gargan. Masses would also have been held in other houses of Catholic aristocracy, like those of the Warrens of Corduff and the Segraves of Little Cabragh. In fact, when the house of the Segraves was demolished in the 1940s a secret room was discovered with a concealed exit. This room would have been used for Mass, with the exit available to help the priest escape should the Penal Laws be enforced.

Henry Luttrell.
Woodcut taken from Cox's Magazine

THE LUTTRELLS DURING THE CIVIL WARS

Simon Luttrell supported Charles I in his struggles with parliament and attended the king's court at Oxford. He was elected to the House of Commons in 1643 and was involved in negotiations between Ormonde and General Preston of the Confederation army. He married into the Gormanstown family – to Mary, the widow of a near neighbour, Sir Thomas Allen of St Wolstan's. Simon died in 1650.

Thomas, Simon's son and heir, suffered because his father backed the losing side in the war. Oliver Cromwell, then lord protector, handed out land in payment for services rendered and gave the Luttrellstown estate to Col John

Hewson, governor of Dublin. Col Hewson had begun his career as a simple shoemaker in Westminster but was later involved with Cromwell in the events that led to Charles I's execution on 30 January 1649. Thomas lived in the stables of Luttrellstown with his wife, Barbara Segrave, of the Cabra Seagraves, until 1655, when he opted for Connaught instead of the much warmer climate Cromwell had in mind for him in a place of no return. The Cromwellian commissioners permitted him to stay on his estate, albeit in the stables. They said of John: 'He showed good affection towards Parliament though not constant good affection.' Sir William Bury, who founded the prestigious line that allied itself with the earls of Charleville, leased the house from Hewson for some of this time. Hewson was obviously a two-faced rascal, receiving knighthoods from first Oliver Cromwell and then Charles II.

On the restoration of the monarchy in 1660, Thomas Luttrell was returned to his estate, which consisted of a great mansion of twelve chimneys, a malt house, a barn and two stables, all slated and valued at the considerable sum of £1,000. The estate also included ornamental gardens, three orchards, two quarries, a corn mill, a cloth mill and a salmon weir. The grange had thatched houses, a second mill, orchard, and about twelve cottages. The whole parish of Clonsilla belonged to Luttrell, except Coolmine, which was Sir Edward Bolton's, and Castaheany, which the Barnewalls owned.

It is believed that the Luttrells' land was restored through the offices of Sir Maurice Berkeley, whose brother Charles, according to Samuel Pepys' *Diary*, 'had the Kings ear'. One of the commissioners deciding on the settlement of the Irish estates was a Winston Churchill, an ancestor of Winston Spencer Churchill, who in turn had connections with the area, as will become clear. It was widely remarked at the time that some people had their lands restored in better condition than when they were seized. Under the 1653 Act of Satisfaction, the Castleknock barony was set aside to satisfy the claims of maimed soldiers and the widows and orphans of soldiers; this was never implemented, however.

Thomas was involved in a curious incident – a duel in which the protagonists emerged unscathed but the seconds were seriously injured. It would appear that the Luttrell family still held to the old faith, as shortly before Thomas died he prevented his son Simon from marrying a Protestant heiress named Legge solely because of her religion. Following Thomas' death in 1673, his son Simon inherited the estate.

THE LUTTRELLS AND TWO KINGS

Both Simon and his brother Henry were educated in France, and their so-journ there did nothing to help form their characters, particularly in the case of Henry. Simon married the daughter of Sir Thomas Newcomen Bart, in whose regiment he was serving as a lieutenant colonel. She was a Protestant, and the couple were married first by a clergyman of the Established Church and later by the bride's uncle, Peter Talbot, Catholic archbishop of Dublin and brother of Richard Talbot, earl of Tyrconnell, who was James II's lord lieutenant. (Tyrconnell was given the nickname 'Lying Dick' by the people).

Simon appears not to have enjoyed good health and was at one time threatened with paralysis. He was a loyal supporter of James II and became lord lieutenant of County Dublin and member of the privy council. He was MP for the county in the Jacobite parliament of 1689 and became military governor of the city. The county was also represented by his neighbour and comrade-in-arms Patrick Sarsfield of Lucan. Simon's brother Henry represented Carlow.

Simon was forced to withdraw from Dublin following the defeat of James' army at the Boyne, and followed James to France, returning in October 1690 with a French fleet, too late to aid the Irish Jacobite cause. He did not avail of the clause in the Treaty of Limerick allowing former Jacobite officers to return and swear allegiance to William and Mary and retain their estates. He served with the French army in Italy and Catalonia and died in 1698. Some sources claim he died with Sarsfield at Landen in 1693, but this is not true, and an inscription in the Irish College, Paris, records his death as 6 September 1698.

Following his refusal to pledge allegiance to King William of Orange and Queen Mary, his estates at Luttrellstown became forfeit and devolved to his brother Henry, who turned his coat and betrayed the Jacobite cause. Without

Members of the Hellfire Club. Left to right: Henry Barry, fourth Lord Santry, Col
Clements, Col Ponsonby, Col St George, Simon Luttrell.
'The Hellfire Club' by James Worsdale', courtesy of the National Gallery of Ireland

in any way reducing the enormity of Henry's treachery, it is worth recalling that many wealthy aristocratic families owed their positions, privilege and indeed wealth in their chameleon-like ability to change their religion, politics and loyalty at the whim of those in power.

William III was son-in-law to James II, his wife, Mary, who was joint ruler with him, being James' elder daughter. Pope Alexander VIII was in dispute with Louis XIV of France, who was an ally of James. As a result, the Pope was delighted with William's victory over James. The Holy Roman Emperor had a *Te Deum* sung in Vienna hailing the Williamite victory at the Boyne. In fact some of the troops in William's army carried the papal insignia into battle. This is a most confusing period, because shortly afterwards Louis recognised William as king, the next pope, Innocent XI, recognised James' succession and that of his heirs and allowed the Stuarts to have a say in the appointments of bishops in Ireland and Great Britain. This arrangement survived until 1766, the year the Old Pretender died. This obviously gave the Williamite succession a reason to doubt Catholic loyalty and was used as the excuse for the implementation of the Penal Laws.

Local folklore relates that after the Boyne, James appeared on horseback galloping down Ballyboggan Road in great haste towards an old Segrave mansion which lay at its junction with Broombridge Road, cursing the cowardly Irish who ran away. A lady he met on the road – in some versions of the story, Lady Tyrconnell – replied, 'I see 'tis your majesty won the race.' The mansion, which was demolished in the early 1970s, was known as King James Castle by all the locals, and Ballyboggan Lane was known as King's Lane. Whether James spent the night there is in doubt, as Dublin Castle would have afforded greater safety; however, the legend is strong and not without support. Incidentally, *The Encyclopaedia Britannica* firmly states that the old style date of the Battle of the Boyne, 1 July 1690, is in effect now 11 July 1690, so are the Orange Order celebrations a day late or could Britannica err?

THE TREACHERY OF HENRY

As a young man in France in 1684, Henry Luttrell, the younger brother of Simon, had engaged in three duels. In one, he killed Lord Purbecke and was injured himself. Lord Macaulay, in his History of England (1848–61), says of him that he 'returned to his native land with a sharpened intellect, polished manners, a flattering tongue, some skill in war and much more skill in intrigue.' Henry returned to Ireland and supported King James and, largely through his efforts, Patrick Sarsfield took Sligo. He earlier conducted himself well at the Battle of the Boyne, albeit he retreated with his dragoons, the Sixth Regiment of Horse. At

Henry Lawes Luttrell, second earl of Carhampton. From a portrait by H.D. Hamilton. Courtesy of the National Gallery of Ireland

the Battle of Aughrim the largest battle ever fought in Ireland, he withdrew his cavalry from the field at a crucial stage and slunk away. Luttrell who was in charge of the reserve cavalry consisting mainly of the French Blue Guards, performed this act of treachery at a place known to this day as 'Luttrell's Pass'. The battle saw seven thousand soldiers killed, three thousand soldiers of William of Orange and four thousand Jacobites. Forty-six thousand soldiers participated in the battle and were evenly divided. It is said that the bodies lay on the battle field for over a year. There was great heroism on both sides but the Jacobites had a major difficulty, as in many cases the ammunition did not fit the muskets. Before the battle, a peddler named Mullin was allowed into the Jacobite camp to sell laces. He spent a long time there, identified General St Ruth's horse, and

Anne Horton (née Luttrell) 1766. Following her husband's death she married the Duke of Cumberland, King George's brother. Painting by Thomas Gainsborough. Courtesy of the National Gallery of Ireland

reported this information back to his spy-master in the Williamite camp. As a result the Williamite gunners were instructed to target St Ruth. One gunner remarked to another 'you have blown off St Ruth's hat', the other replied 'that I have, but you will find his head inside it.' So it was and St Ruth's death finally settled the matter in favour of the Williamites.

During the Siege of Limerick, Luttrell was court-martialled for treachery, having given the enemy information about a vital ford on the Shannon. It appears that his family connections – his brother Simon and the fact that members of the Luttrell family had inter-married with their near neigh-bours the Lucan Sarsfields – saved his life. It is a curious fact that the name Patrick as a Christian name was very rare until Patrick Sarsfield's rise to fame; it is only since then the name became popular.

Henry Luttrell then became involved in supplying soldiers to fight for the Venetian Republic and later became a major general in the Dutch army. The fact that he prevented his sister-in-law, Simon's widow, from gaining her rightful inheritance, together with his notorious debauchery, caused him to be universally detested. The Devil's Mill on the banks of the Liffey at Luttrellstown was, according to local legend, a place of assignation between Henry Luttrell and the devil.

Street ballads were sung about him, poking fun at him for his numerous mistresses and the children he fathered on the wrong side of the blanket. Finally, fate caught up with him; he was fatally wounded by a pistol shot in the autumn of 1717 as he returned home in his sedan chair from the Lucas Coffee House at Cork Hill en route to his Stafford Street town house. His assassins were never apprehended, partly because so many people and factions had motives for killing him. Hardiman penned the following epitaph for Luttrell on his earthly departure:

> If heav'n be pleased when mortals cease to sin
> And hell be pleased when villains enter in,
> If earth be pleased when it entombs a knave
> All must be pleased now Luttrell's in his grave.

Even in death, the hatred he engendered and the loathing his family attracted caused persons unknown to violate his tomb and smash his skull with a pickaxe during the 1798 rebellion. Henry appears to have converted to the Established Church on his deathbed and directed that his sons be brought up as Protestants. This may have had more to do with the laws of inheritance which penalised Catholic families than any genuine religious convictions, but who can say.

Henry left two sons, Richard and Simon. Richard inherited the estate but died within ten years and Simon succeeded him. Simon was raised to the peerage as Baron Irnham and later Earl of Carhampton. His daughter Ann married Henry Fredrick, duke of Cumberland, George III's brother. His son Temple

Luttrell was imprisoned in Paris during the French Revolution on the mistaken view that he was the king's brother rather than his brother-in-law. Lord Carhampton was much involved in political intrigue and corruption. He spent a great deal of his time in Cornwall, where he held a parliamentary seat, and was involved also in Lancashire politics.

In the letters of 'Junius' (1769–71), there is a description of the Luttrells:

> there is a certain family in this country on which nature seems to have entailed a hereditary baseness of disposition. As far as their history has been known the son has regularly improved upon the vices of his father and has taken care to transmit them pure and undiminished into the bosom of his successor.

THE HELL FIRE CLUB

The first Lord Carhampton was a member of the Hellfire Club and features in a painting of a group of five members of this club by James Worsdale in the National Art Gallery. There is a local legend that Luttrell sold his soul to the devil and some years later, while he was engaged in cards with some of these wild young bucks, the devil came to collect. There was a wild scatter for the door and Luttrell was last out, but on fleeing he observed the candlelight throw his shadow large against the wall. Being a shrewd one to the last, he tricked the devil by pointing at the shadow and exclaiming, 'There's Luttrell!' The devil grabbed for the shadow and Luttrell escaped. To this day, none of his descendants casts a shadow – or so the story goes.

The usual meeting place of the Hellfire Club was at Cork Hill near City Hall and not the building on Montpelier Hill in the Dublin mountains. The club members' favourite tipple was a drink called Scaltheen, which was a concoction of melted butter and whiskey. They obviously had devilish tastes and a hellish disrespect for good whiskey.

THE 1798 REBELLION

Simon's son Henry Lawes Luttrell, whose middle name is taken from his

mother Maria, the daughter of Sir Nicholas Lawes, governor of Jamaica, became the second earl of Carhampton on his father's death in 1787.

Henry Lawes Luttrell was a soldier and politician and rose to a high position in the army, becoming adjutant general of the land forces in Ireland.
During the events that culminated in the 1798 Rebellion he press-ganged suspected rebels from Westmeath, Leitrim, Longford and Roscommon into the
navy. The degree of evidence used in establishing suspects was nil – the whim
of a landlord was enough.

Lord Camden, the lord lieutenant, wrote that Carhampton did not confine
himself to the strict rule of law. This did not prevent parliament from passing
an act indemnifying him from exceeding the limits of the law. On the 25 May
1797 James Dunne, a farmer and blacksmith, and Patrick Carthy, a labourer,
both workers on the Luttrellstown estate, set up an assassination attempt on
Lord Carhampton but were betrayed by a man named Ferris and were both
hanged. Carhampton's activities were intended to prevent the 1798 Rebellion.
His brutal actions however did more to provoke it.

THE LAST OF THE LUTTRELLS

Shortly after this, Henry Lawes, the last of the Luttrells of Luttrellstown, decamped for his English estates at Painshill in Surrey, where he died in 1821.
An amusing anecdote about him is worth relating: In the Dublin Post of 2 May
1811, the death of Henry Lawes Luttrell was reported. Luttrell, being very
much alive, contacted the newspaper in foul temper, demanding a retraction.
The issue of the 5 May 1811 corrected their earlier death notice, confirming
that Luttrell was alive and well under the heading 'Public Disappointment.'
His brother John, who succeeded him, died in 1829, at which time the title
became extinct.

Henry Lawes Luttrell had a natural son, Henry, because of an affair with a
gardener's daughter from Woodstock. The son was a renowned society wit and
poet and was an associate of Thomas Moore, Lord Macaulay, Lady Blessington
and Lord Byron. He died in 1851, aged 86. Another family member, James,

The Devil's Mill near Luttrellstown, 1795
Courtesy Fingal County Council

Luttrellstown Castle in 1996
Courtesy of the Primwest Group

gave distinguished service in the navy, capturing American prize ships during the war between Britain and the United States.

Lady Ann, the Duke of Cumberland's wife, had a reputation for using her undoubted beauty – Gainsborough and Reynolds painted her – to good advantage, and Horace Walpole described her as having 'eyelashes half a yard long as a coquette beyond measure.' Indeed she was a widow when she lured the duke of Cumberland into a marriage, which his brother George III opposed so bitterly that they had to be married in Calais. Such was the king's anger that he subsequently enacted a law preventing those in the royal succession from marrying without the permission of the monarch. The law is still on the statute books and enforced to this day. Lady Ann's sister, Lady Elizabeth, lost money at gambling tables and was imprisoned for debt. She married one of her servants – her hairdresser – and thus transferred her debts to him. She turned up in Augsburg some time later, where she was convicted of picking pockets. She died after poisoning herself.

Thus ends the 500 plus years association of the Luttrell family with Clonsilla. Some of this association was good, some was bad, although towards the end of the line there were some odious characters. Perhaps Henry Lawes Luttrell should have the final word. When his father, Simon, challenged him to a duel, he declined on the grounds that: 'It was not given by a gentleman.'

THE QUEEN SHE CAME TO CALL ON US

The estate, although vacated by Luttrell in 1798, does not appear to have been sold until 1811. The new owner was a Luke White, a native of the Isle of Man, who achieved great wealth by a means that is still employed today – the lottery. The Dominican friar Savonarola in the fifteenth century, described the lottery as a tax on stupidity. Wasn't Luke White a right oul' eejit to end up with a beautiful demesne like Luttrellstown? Well, apparently he was a seller of lottery tickets. There is a story told that he rode after the mail coach to Belfast and bought unsold tickets, as he suspected that the winning numbers were in that pile; evidently he was correct and made a fortune.

White was originally a bookseller, and even today Luttrellstown Castle has a fine library. He changed the name of the estate to Woodlands because of the bad reputation of Luttrellstown. The name Woodlands appears on maps but was never used locally, as the people of the area firmly said: 'Fair or foul, Luttrellstown it is.'

White bought the estate for £180,000. Luttrell tried to renege on the deal because White was not of the aristocracy and offered his money back plus £40.000; White declined the offer. He became High Sheriff for Dublin in 1804 and MP for Leitrim between 1812 and 24.

In or about the year 1820 Prince Von Puckler–Muskau visited Luttrellstown Castle and this is how he described it 'The entrance to the demesne is indeed the most delightful in its kind that can be imagined. Scenery, by nature most beautiful, is improved by art to the highest degree of its capability, and, without destroying its free and wild character, a variety of richness of vegetation is produced which enchants the eye. Gay shrubs and wild flowers, the softest turf and giant trees, festooned with creeping plants, fill the narrow glen through which the path winds, by the side of the clear, dancing brook, which, falling in little cataracts, flows on, sometimes hidden in the thicket, sometimes resting like liquid silver in an emerald cup, or rushing under overhanging arches of rock, which nature seems to have hung there as triumphal gates for the beneficient Naiad of the valley to pass through.'

In August 1849 the thirty-year old Queen Victoria, on her visit to Ireland, paid a call on the duke of Leinster at Carton House and dropped into Luttrellstown on the way. She wore a green Irish poplin dress embroidered with gold shamrocks. This was just shortly after the worst ravages of the famine were beginning to abate. She is said to have donated £5 for famine relief in Ireland and, fearing that she would be accused of favouritism, gave £5 to Battersea Dogs Home on the same day. This story is not true. She was in fact reasonably generous for her times; she donated a substantial amount of her own money to famine relief. Her ministers and government officials, on the other hand, were more interested in bookkeeping and preserving laissez-faire economics than in preserving human life.

In 1863 Henry White, the incumbent, who served and was decorated in the Peninsular War, was created Lord Annaly, and in January the following year there were two weeks of celebration at Luttrellstown to commemorate the event. In April 1900, Queen Victoria dropped in to Luttrellstown for a longer visit; where she took tea in the Glen at a spot that is marked today by an obelisk eight and a half feet tall. Nora Comiskey whose father was a worker on the estate recalled the many times it had to be retrieved from the adjoining lake following the high jinks of local lads. This visit was to record her appreciation to the Irish soldiers who had performed sterling work in the British army, particularly in the Boer War.

The 'younger' Lord Annaly, circa 1890s.
Courtesy of Vanity Fair

One of her entourage is said to have engaged a member of an old Irish family in conversation and, wishing to impress, remarked that he could trace his family tree back to 1600. The impressed Irishman remarked that so could he: 1600 bc! He said he was descended from Milesian princes. In fact, the British royal family have a fair amount of Irish blood in their veins and can trace bloodlines back to Brian Boru.

TALES OUT OF SCHOOL

Local folklore has a story about Lord Annaly refusing the local priest land for building a school. The story goes that the old national school in Porterstown was built high in an attempt to annoy him when he saw it. In fact, Lord Annaly was generous to both churches in the locality and gave land for the church. He built, endowed and supported a school beside the old Catholic chapel in Porterstown (later the Scouts Den). He placed the school under the management of Fr Myles McPharlan, PP (1803–25).

Old entrance gate to Luttrellstown Castle including Hogan's Gate Lodge
viewed from the front
Photograph by Fr Eugene Kennedy

A struggle subsequently developed between the Protestant and the Catholic clergy concerning the management of the school. Col White seemed to favour the Kildare Place Society as managers. In the end, five years after the school was built, White gave the former school house to Fr Dungan on condition it be used for Roman Catholic purposes.

Two stories about Lord Annaly have done the rounds for years. In one he dies of apoplexy when his butler points out the flag flying from the chimney of the new school. In fact, the school was built in 1853–54, nine years before Col White was made Lord Annaly. He lived for a further ten years.

The other story is that the priest cursed the land, saying 'a crow would never build a nest, a ewe would never lamb and a hare would never run on it.' Yarns like these make good and entertaining reading but are unfair to the memory of a man who, whatever other faults he may have had, was more generous than most of his class and in fact behaved in a fashion directly opposite to what the stories relate.

STRAWBERRY FIELDS – FOR A WHILE

It was during this period that much of the tree planting on and renovation of the estate took place. The walled gardens were famous for growing peaches; in fact the whole area, as gardeners will confirm, was ideal for growing fruit trees, in particular the prunus species – greengages, damsons and plums – of which peach (*Prunus Persica*) is a tender variety. Col White appears to have started intensive strawberry cultivation along the slopes of Astagob and down to the lower road. As well as Luttrellstown, he owned Astagob and part of Porterstown. (The other part was the property of a Miss Locke, who also cultivated strawberries; she owned property in Carpenterstown as well). This cultivation of strawberries is commemorated to this day in the area known as the Strawberry Beds.

The West brothers were noted for their excellent crops. The 560 acres (2,139 acres in 1876) of demesne, with its man-made lake, enchanting waterfall and sparkling stream tumbling down to the Liffey, make for a fairy wonderland. Lord Annaly sold the estate in 1919 and the family moved to Holdenby House Northamptonshire.

MODERN TIMES

The new owner, a Major Hamilton, lived only three years after acquiring the estate, and his widow sold it in 1930 to Arthur Ernest Guinness, brother of Lord Iveagh, who gave it as a wedding present to his daughter Aileen on her marriage to Brinsley Plunkett. An airman, Plunkett was killed in the Second World War. The Italian Embassy leased the estate during the war until they moved to the De Vesci estate which formerly belonged to Patrick Sarsfield's family.

In 1954 Luttrellstown Castle was the location for the film The Black Knight, starring Alan Ladd. Doon Plunkett, daughter of Aileen and Brinsley Plunkett, married Lord Granville, first cousin to Elizabeth II, and decided that, as they were unlikely to settle there, they would sell the estate to the Primwest Group. Since then, the castle has been lavishly restored; and its fourteen exquisitely furnished rooms can now be viewed by paying guests. There are four reception rooms, a magnificent ballroom and facilities for swimming, tennis, fishing, shooting and golfing on one of the finest championship courses in the country. There are also self-catering stable-yard apartments with their own unique ambience. The clubhouse is entirely built of timber and is the largest wooden building in Ireland. Some of the most recent visitors to Luttrellstown include the late President Reagan, Prince Rainier and Princess Grace of Monaco; the grand duke of Luxembourg, the king and queen of Denmark, a myriad of stars from stage and screen and various sporting legends. Luttrellstown is continuing to make its own history. Soccer star David Beckham and Victoria Adams of Spice Girl fame tied the nuptial knot here. The celebrant of the marriage was the Rev. Paul Colton, rector of Castleknock. He is now bishop of Cork, Cloyne and Ross. The castle and demesne again changed hands in 2006 and is now owned by a consortium consisting of J.P. McManus, John Magnier and Aidan Brooks.

3

CLONSILLA

The manifest influence Luttrellstown exerted on Clonsilla and its environs in no way hindered the other developments – agricultural, social, ecclesiastical and mysterious – that took place there. The place name Clonsilla (Cluain Saileach – 'the sally meadow') refers to the willows (salix in Latin) that grew on the margins of the Great Scaldwood.

The word cluain means not only 'meadow' but also a 'place of peace or retreat,' such as would be expected near a monastery or abbey. In fact there is medicinal value in willows; this was known by people close to nature such as American Indians, who chewed the leaves and bark of the trees. Maybe the monks of yore knew of this and used products from these trees along with other medicinal herbs they

St Mary's church, Clonsilla
Photograph by Fr Eugene Kennedy

grew in their monastery gardens. Salicylic acid, used in the manufacture of aspirin and wintergreen (a fungicide treatment), are both derived from sally bushes and the spiraea plant.

The area of Clonsilla has been associated from early times with St Mochta, who was a follower of St Patrick. There are many legends relating to St Mochta; in one he restored life to a thief condemned to death by King Ailil. The thief was drowned with the proverbial millstone around his neck. When the grieving parents pleaded with St Mochta, however, he raised the thief from the dead. The thief repented and became a disciple of St Mochta. In another story, while travelling on his apostolic work with his monks St Mochta discovered that two of the monks' horses had been stolen. In spite of the fact that the thieves galloped on the horses all night, they had hardly moved the next morning; they were stuck to the saddlery until they repented and the saint absolved them. St Mochta also has a particular association with Louth and appears to have spent much of his time there until his death in 534.

The church he built – in Coolmine, to the rear of what is now Coolmine Community School – was known as the White Church. It was in a ruinous state even in 1419 and there is now not a trace of it left. The church is commemorated in the name Whitechapel, which was given to the adjoining area.

Annefield House, birthplace of Dr Troy in 1739
Photograph by Fr Eugene Kennedy

CLONSILLA'S CHRISTIAN HERITAGE

The Tyrell family particularly favoured the Benedictine abbey of Little Malvern in Worcestershire barons of Castleknock, who originally settled in that area following the Norman Conquest of England. When the Tyrells extended their possessions to Ireland they helped found Benedictine houses at Castleknock and Clonsilla as dependent priories of Little Malvern. In about 1215, Henry de Londres, archbishop of Dublin, consecrated the priory of St Brigid's Clonsilla. This eventually replaced the Celtic foundation of St Mochta in Coolmine and today is the site of a fine Church of Ireland church.

These monks of Little Malvern also held the priory of St Brigid (now Castleknock parish church of St Brigid), along with lands and a mill on the Liffey. Monasteries owned half of Worcestershire, where they had their main house, and the monks' remains are scattered along the Malvern Hills and valleys. The name Malvern comes from the ancient British Celtic language meaning 'bald hill.'

The lands and priory were transferred to the ownership of St Mary's Abbey in 1486 and on the dissolution of the monasteries with Henry VIII's break with Rome, became the property of the Luttrell family. The church still held the title of St Machutus (Mochta), as can be seen in deeds transferred at that time. The present Church of Ireland building was rebuilt in 1846 and was consecrated by Archbishop Whately. Its bells were originally in St Werburgh's church and were taken down when the spire was removed owing to the fact that it overlooked Dublin Castle and therefore possibly afforded a position from which to fire into the castle.

ARCHBISHOP FITZSIMONS

The churchyard is the last resting place of members of the Luttrell family, the White family and at least one Roman Catholic archbishop, Dr Patrick Fitzsimons, who died in 1770. Around the time of his death, all Roman Catholics were buried in Protestant churchyards or pre-Reformation graveyards owing to the Penal Laws. It is conjectured that the Archbishop of Dublin, Peter Talbot, who died in 1680, may be buried with or near his sister Lady Newcomen, whose daughter married Col Simon Luttrell. As this was a difficult time for people professing Roman Catholicism, the details of his death and internment are scant.

Though the location of his last resting place is unrecorded, the archbishop was likely to have been laid to rest beside his kin in Clonsilla. Dr Fitzsimon's tombstone on the other hand, records his death on 25 November 1769 aged seventy-one. He was the son of Richard Fitzsimon who died on 5 October 1736 aged seventy-seven. Patrick Fitzsimon was parish priest of St Paul's cathedral in London when he was elevated to the position of archbishop in 1763. He had previously been chaplain to the Spanish ambassador; the fact that he had been educated in Spain was of considerable advantage to him. His mother was Bridget Moore, who died in 1741 aged seventy-three. Coincidentally, he was born next door to Archbishop Troy's birthplace at Annefield, in a house, long since gone, that was sited in St Mochta's playing fields and is now known locally as 'the bishop's field.'

THE CROWN JEWELS

About the time of the visit of Edward VII in July 1907, an event occurred that gave rise to rumours of another burial in Clonsilla churchyard. A big search was carried out in Clonsilla graveyard for the 'Irish crown jewels.' These were in fact the regalia of the Order of St Patrick founded in 1783. The regalia were presented to the order in 1831 by King William IV and consisted of a Grand Masters Star and Badges encrusted with emeralds, rubies and diamonds as well as collarettes. Today's value of these items would be in excess of €3.5 million euro.

The jewels 'walked' from the secure environs of Dublin Castle in July 1907 just days before the royal visit of King Edward VII. The king was furious and a huge investigation was launched into their theft.

The Ulster King of Arms, Sir Arthur Vicars, the principal herald of Ireland, i.e. the most senior genealogist who was also the custodian of the jewels came under suspicion, as did Frank Shackleton – Dublin herald (who was, incidentally, a brother of the famous Antarctic explorer Sir Ernest Shackleton), Francis Bennett-Goldney Athlone Pursuivant and Pierce Gun-Mahony Cork Herald.

The search for the crown jewels was conducted through the length and breadth of the country. Sir William Harrell, assistant commissioner DMP took charge. Chief Inspector Kane of Scotland Yard was assigned to the case and Sir Anthony MacDonnell as permanent under secretary, probably the most powerful government official at the time, personally became involved.

At one stage Sir Arthur Conan Doyle the creator of the Sherlock Holmes character and also a believer in spiritualism and mediums and coincidentally a relative of Vicars, recommended a clairvoyant who said she saw the jewels buried beside the gate at an old disused graveyard near Clonsilla.

The police descended on the churchyard of St Mary's Clonsilla and as the newspapers of the time relate found nothing 'but dank nettles and cow parsley'. Incidentally, the churchyard at Clonsilla was not disused at that time and is presently still accepting burials. Some local interest followed and much soil was turned over resulting in blisters and callouses and little else.

Sir Arthur Vicars became the scapegoat and was fired from office. Most commentators lay the blame with Frank Shackleton who was a cousin of his namesake the Shackleton's of Beech Park – not a stone's throw from St Mary's churchyard. However, Frank Shackleton never appeared to have lived in Beech Park or would have been that familiar with the area.

Vicars had homosexual leanings as did most of the senior genealogists and had contacts with Lord Hatton, son of the lord lieutenant. A Capt. Gorges was alleged to have assisted Shackleton in the theft.

When the scandal began to reach towards the royal family through the inclusion of the duke of Argyll's name (he was married to a sister of the king and was a promiscuous bi-sexual), in the imbroglio a halt was called to the investigation.

It has to be remembered, at the time, homosexuality, (amongst men), was a most serious crime in the eyes of the law, meriting a substantial prison sentence and social disgrace. I say amongst men because, when the bill was being drafted, Queen Victoria could not comprehend how females could possibly indulge in such a vice so it was redrafted to exclude ladies.

Because of the legal situation and the social mores prevailing at that time, gay men were vulnerable to blackmail and intimidation. Therefore, anyone wishing to pocket the jewels and having knowledge of the intimate lifestyles of those involved had an easy entrée – to the jewels that is.

Pierce Gun-Mahony died in 1914 following a shooting accident. Francis Bennett-Goldney died in 1918 following a motor accident. Sir Arthur Vicars died in 1921 shot by the IRA and Capt. Gorges threw himself under a tram. Shackleton was never charged with any crime relating to the crown jewels but served an eighteen-month sentence for fraudulent conversion six years later relating to another incident. He died of natural causes in 1941.

The following organisations have been accused of stealing the crown jewels – the Bolsheviks to fund the Russian Revolution, the Irish Republican Brotherhood to fund an Irish Revolution, the Unionists to discredit the Home Rule inclined administration in Dublin, the king to pay a blackmailer, etc., etc. Suffice to say from time to time stories of the location of the jewels surface – 1927, 1950, 1983 and 1996. However, that's all that surfaces – stories.

Given the astronomical prices we see developers are willing to pay for land in the area it strikes me that the real treasure was the land being dug up and cast aside in pursuit of the illusion!

In 1935, a stained-glass window of St Fiacre by Evie Hone, the eminent stained glass artist, was installed to enhance this lovely church.

BLOODSTOCK

The Clonsilla area is rich in limestone and has from time immemorial been used for horse breeding. During the Great War, the area supplied an immense quantity of horses for the British army. A type of workhorse called a 'trooper', used for pulling gun carriages, was particularly prized. These horses were paddocked in fields close to the railway station. Apparently, an officer would sit at a table in the field adjoining the station, flanked by a pay clerk, as he watched the horses being put through their paces, usually by a local horseman named Smith. Fields at Manley's, and later Brady's, farm at Laurel Lodge were used for rest and recuperation for these war horses. Maxie Arnott (of the Arnott family of Henry Street fame), along with Capt. Delhurst of Greenmount House and Cottage, Clonsilla, bred and trained racehorses successfully. This business gave much employment in the area.

A party of armed men burnt Capt. Delhurst's residence in 1923. Mr William Steed's property, Clonsilla House, was also burned on the same occasion. Steed was a racehorse owner too. His father had had difficulty with the Land League years before. In 1887, several of his horses died from arsenic poisoning; the culprits were never discovered. Another famed horseman was Michael Betagh of Lohunda House, which was named after a place in India where he saw service and barely escaped with his life during the Indian mutiny.

AROUND CLONSILLA'S LEAFY LANES

The section of Clonsilla Road from where it adjoins Porterstown Road leading to the church at Clonsilla is recent. The road originally went around by Porterstown and Luttrellstown back over the canal to the road for Clonee. Orchard Avenue, or Weavers Row, a name derived from the hand-weaving tradition in the locality, was given the nickname 'Sprout Alley' because of the intensive cultivation of brussels sprouts there. The residents did not take to the name with the same alacrity as those in the lower road took to the name 'Strawberry Beds.' At the old entrance to Lohunda Demesne, opposite Lambourne Estate, there was a tradition of a regular haunting by a headless apparition.

On the corner of Luttrellstown Demesne adjoining the Rugged Lane, there are the remains of a castellated gatehouse known as Hogan's Lodge. Three people lived in these two small towers. One Paddy Hogan was six foot four inches and in order to go upstairs was obliged to go outside to climb the exterior staircase to the cramped accommodation above. An old chapel is shown here in the Rocque Map of 1760; it was later moved to Kellystown.

The Rugged Lane was so called because of its ruts and potholes. There is a story that so many sheep went up and down it that their wool, clinging to the briars there, made it seem like a long rug. I feel, however, that this story applies more to the Woolly Corner, a place at the top of Somerton Hill where sheep gathered on their way to market. A more colourful story relating to the Rugged Lane concerns the names of the residents there – Messrs White, Black, and Brown, respectively. Since I wrote the above some years ago, I have remembered that what I described as colours are, in fact, shapes. So, with that new light on the matter, it is now a shady story. Halfway down this lane there is a house and lands called Pilgrims Land. There was speculation that the name came from returning crusaders. The simple truth is that a previous owner was Joe Pilgrim. There are stone, toadstool-shaped objects at the entrance that often give rise to comment. These were used in harvesting crops so that when the rick or stack was made, the bottom stood on the toadstool, allowing air circulation and a measure of protection from rodents. They are more commonly used in Co. Wicklow.

ARCHBISHOP TROY

Preacher, prelate and pastor, archbishop of Dublin 1786–1823

John Thomas Troy was born in Annefield House, Porterstown on 10 May 1739, the son of a prosperous hotelier and landowner. While still a youth, he enlisted with the Order of Preachers (the Dominicans) and was sent to Rome where he studied and was ordained at 22 years of age.

His diaries reveal little of his personality but did show evidence of an enquiring mind, a very ordered and regimented nature and an awareness of class. His diaries also indicate that he was of an extremely parsimonious disposition, listing prices and items in great detail. In contradiction to this, on his death he had only one guinea in his pocket and little other possessions, having given most to the poor.

During his period in Rome, he was rector of San Clemente and drew the favourable attention of his superiors. He was consecrated in Louvain as bishop of Ossory in 1786. Ten years later, he was appointed to the Dublin diocese as archbishop on the death of his cousin the previous incumbent Dr John Carpenter.

This was a precarious time for Roman Catholics, particularly clergy. The Penal Laws were at times implemented with full rigor so an immense degree of tact and diplomacy was necessary.

John Thomas Troy, archbishop of Dublin 1786-1823
Portrait by Thomas Clement Thompson, courtesy of the National Gallery of Ireland

The government included Lords Castlereagh, Clare and Clonmel who were steeped in bigotry and needed little or no reason to exercise the draconian powers available to them. This was a time of revolution in America followed by France and other countries of continental Europe. Ireland, like other countries, was stirred by these events. The United Irishmen were organising, the White Boys, the Defenders and the Orange Order were all active. During the 1798 Rising, ghastly atrocities were perpetrated by both sides and non-combatants were often as likely to be killed as those in the thick of battle.

Dr Troy had negotiated a pact with the British government, which culminated in the foundation of Maynooth College in 1795 for the education of seminarians to the priesthood, to be funded by State monies. The *quid pro quo* was that the British government would have a say and a veto in the appointment of Irish bishops.

During the French Revolution the Roman Catholic church, its clergy and its property were as likely to be attacked as the monarchy and nobility. Dr Troy feared a similar revolution in Ireland could result in turmoil for his beloved church, at a time when he was slowly wringing concessions from Westminster. The British government feared that priests educated on the continent might import revolutionary ideas into the country. Dr Troy was from gentry stock and was an arch conservative by nature, indeed as bishop of Ossory he had urged a day of prayer and fasting so that the American colonies might stay within the king's realm.

Clearly, the government and the church had common cause. For his part, Troy thought conciliation might ameliorate the conditions of the Catholic population. He was not political nor even pretended sympathy for Irish nationalism but was solely a churchman. It was said that Maynooth seminary was worth more to King George than several regiments of cavalry and cheaper to maintain. Dr Troy, however, did plead many times on behalf of individual prisoners and urged restraint following the defeat of the 1798 insurgents.

Despite his support for government, he was distrusted. Lord Chancellor Redsdale fulminated 'Maynooth vomits out priests ten times worse than ever came from the Spanish colleges. I would withdraw supplies to this establishment and if I were Minister I would abolish it.' At this time, when Dr Troy was preaching 'Fear God, honour the King, obey and respect your superiors of every description', and describing the handful of his clergy that were involved in the 1798 Rebellion as 'the very faeces of the church.'

Troy supported the Act of Union and encouraged the Irish hierarchy to row in behind him along with their flock on the understanding from Prime Minister Pitt that it would bring about Catholic emancipation. Ironically, the Orange Order disapproved of the Act of Union with scores of Lodges passing resolutions against it. When the Act of Union was passed, King George refused to sign the bill granting emancipation saying that it would violate his Coronation Oath and Pitt resigned.

With the passing of time, the Penal Laws and the implementation of them were relaxed until Catholic emancipation happened in 1829.

On a personal level, he was noted for his hospitality but was extremely abstemious himself. He was regaled everywhere for his fine wine cellar particularly his sack – a very popular wine of that era. Lord Norbury, the hanging judge, noticed Eneas McDonnell, editor of the *Catholic Chronicle*, leaving the archbishop's house on Cavendish Row, and he remarked to a colleague, 'There goes the pious Eneas coming from the sack of Troy.'

In the 1790s, there was a move among priests for optional celibacy and election of clergy by the laity in the Dublin dioceses! Fr Robert McEvoy in Swords got married and insisted he remain in the ministry. Troy immediately excommunicated him, crushing the 'French mania,' as this Catholic reformation was called.

It is interesting to note that in 1815, at the laying of the foundation stone of the pro-cathedral, the Dean of Christchurch, prominent Dissenters, Quakers and Orangemen attended; the Guinnesses and Daniel O'Connell were also present. Doctor Troy died on 11 May 1823; his death was announced in the *Freeman's Journal* as follows:

DEATH OF THE CATHOLIC ARCHBISHOP OF DUBLIN
The venerable, learned and pious Doctor John Thomas Troy, Roman Catholic Archbishop of Dublin, died at his residence in Cavendish Row, on Saturday evening, after an illness of some weeks. He was a bishop forty-seven years and filled the Metropolitan See Thirty Seven. Doctor Troy was born in the city of Dublin, in July 1739, appointed bishop in December 1776, consecrated the following year, 1777, and translated to the Archdiocese of Dublin 1786. Doctor Troy possessed a sound understanding, extensive information and great virtue. The whole of his long life was exclusively devoted to the duties of his sacred calling. He was aged 83 years and ten months. As a mark of respect to his memory, it has been resolved that his funeral shall be a public one.

As the pro-cathedral was unfinished, he was not interred there until 1825. Dr Troy was the last Catholic archbishop to retain the old feudal title of baron in his description. His many pieces of plate have a baron's coronet added to the ecclesiastical hat, and there are tassels on his coat of arms.

The Troy's family tomb is in the long disused local graveyard of Caeveen, some hundreds of yards across the Tolka River from the Total Fitness complex. His brother Walter Troy appears to have been the last of the family to be interred there.

ARCHBISHOP CARPENTER

Dr Carpenter, Dr Troy's predecessor, was archbishop from 1770 to 1786; he was a cousin of Dr Troy and left the lease of his house on Usher's Island and a topaz ring to his cousin Catherine Troy. He was born in Chancery Lane in 1729 to a family associated with Carpenterstown but he never lived there. His father was a wealthy merchant tailor. He was not able to speak until he witnessed a horrific accident at the age of seven. His missal was preserved in Blanchardstown church for years. His inscription, as an eminent Irish scholar, was as follows:

> Do leabhraimh Séain Mhic an Tshair, Ard-Easpog Átha Cliath Dubhlin agus Primhaid Érinn agus do coisríogadh don tSúidh sin an triú la do Jún MDCCLXX.

During Dr Carpenter's tenure of office the Penal Laws were enforced more harshly than in his successor Dr Troy's time. Catholic schools were illegal but many existed and were only intermittently interfered with. Priests, however, had to be very discreet and 'Mass Houses, Nunneries, Fryers and Popish schools that might be found' were to be accounted for and returned by 'the Lord Mayor, the Seneschals of the different Liberties and by the Ministers and Churchwardens.' It was also forbidden for Mass Houses to have steeples or bells.

The young John Carpenter attended Tadhg O'Neachtain's all Irish speaking school where he also studied English and Latin among other subjects. O'Neachtain was a well-known lexicographer, poet, historian and translator. In fact, O'Neachtain's school was more of an Irish speaking academy than a school. It was from these roots that Dr Carpenter's love of the Irish language grew.

John Carpenter left for Lisbon at eighteen years of age and studied for the priesthood in the Irish College there, where he was also ordained. His first appointment was to St Mary's chapel in Liffey Street. Some time afterwards he was called on to act as secretary to Count Taaffe, an Irish born Austrian field marshal. Count Taaffe was visiting King George III in an effort to persuade the king to make concessions to the Catholic people in Ireland. They had several interviews with the king but achieved nothing.

Fr Carpenter was consecrated archbishop of Dublin on June 3, 1770, and took over St Nicholas of Myra parish as his mensal parish.

In 1774, parliament drew up an oath of fealty, which if taken, would give Catholics limited legal status and recognise them as citizens allowing basic rights such as the ability to take out a mortgage. This oath incorporated a clause denying the pope's temporal power but Dr Carpenter reserved his decision until Rome agreed with the oath. He subscribed to the oath along with seventy of his clergy and 1,250 traders and merchants.

It is probably not well known that Dublin in the mid to late 1700s and early 1800s was not noted as a city devoted to church services and mass going. The Catholics of the city at that time like many today were baptised, married and buried with Catholic church rites or as they say – hatched, matched and dispatched but mass attendances were of the order of fifty percent. There was a lot of indifference and apathy particularly among the poor who set great store by holy wells and holy bushes and waking the dead but who were little exercised by formal ritual. Dr Troy, in his time, issued instructions that non-churchgoers would be denied a Christian marriage, be refused permission to act as godparents nor would they be given the church blessing after childbirth. However, he did accord them Christian burial.

Dr Carpenter addressed the faithful on Christmas Day 1772, condemning the laxity of those eating meat on Friday and Saturday during the Christmas period. He emphasised that, like the rest of the year, Fridays as well as Saturdays and Wednesdays were days of abstinence from meat under pain of mortal sin. He died on the 29 of October 1786 and is buried in the tomb of his brother-in-law, Thomas Lee, in St Michan's churchyard.

CLONSILLA'S FAMOUS JUDGE

Clonsilla's famous judge was mentioned in James Joyce's *Ulysses*. He was a member of the legal team that prosecuted the 1916 leaders. He was legal advisor to the Dublin Castle administration before the Truce that ended the War of Independence. He was a founder member of the Irish Red Cross, a high court judge during the British administration, and remained on the bench when the Irish Free State emerged. The Hon. Judge William Wylie, KC, had a history. In fact he was part of history.

Judge W.E. Wylie, formerly of Clonsilla House

William Evelyn Wylie was born in Dublin in 1881, the son of a County Derry Presbyterian minister. He was called to the bar in 1905. During his time at Trinity College, he became involved in cycle racing – a sport then in its infancy and it was in this context that Joyce mentioned him in *Ulysses*.

He had a successful legal practice, took silk in 1914, and was hailed as one of the foremost advocates of the time. He joined the Territorial Army in 1915 where he was attached to the Officer Training Corps in Trinity College.

When the Easter Rising broke out, he was on holiday in Kerry with his wife Ida. When he returned to Upper Fitzwilliam Street in Dublin his then home, he reported to Pembroke town hall where the Inniskilling Fusiliers were ensconced. He took no active part in the fighting but was delegated the task of interviewing captured prisoners. He was summoned to General Byrne's office when the Rebellion ended where he was given the unenviable task of prosecuting the 1916 leaders.

He was much impressed by the men who appeared before the court, particularly Pearse. He mentioned in his memoirs that General Blackadder, the presiding officer at the court-martial, suggested that the names printed on the Easter Proclamation could be used as evidence of the signatories part in the direction of the rebellion. Wylie pointed out that the names were merely printed and as it was not a signature, it was not proof.

Wylie also thought that Thomas Clarke, who did not offer any defence, was calm and brave throughout his court martial and struck him as being a particularly kindly man. Wylie did his best to postpone James Connolly's court martial because of Connolly's injuries but was not successful. He was withdrawn as prosecution counsel in Connolly's trial, possibly for this reason. Had Wylie's attempt to postpone Connolly's trial succeeded it may have saved him. By the time he

Wintry Scene at the twelfth lock, Blanchardstown.
Photograph by Jim Lacey

and Seán MacDermot were shot, Prime Minister Asquith had already instructed General Maxwell, military supremo in Dublin, to cease the executions.

Wylie was critical of one person – Countess Markievicz who, in his words, 'curled up completely'. According to Wylie, she cried out in court 'you cannot shoot a woman, you must not shoot a woman.' The official transcripts of her trial do not record this outburst in court. Wylie's writing is free of rancour and bias and one cannot explain why he relates this story if it is not true.

Wylie maintained that Éamon de Valera's American citizenship was not mentioned during his court martial. General Maxwell showed Asquith's telegram curtailing the executions and asked who was next on the list. 'Somebody called de Valera sir,' replied Wylie. 'I wonder would he be likely to make trouble in the future?' queried Maxwell. 'I wouldn't think so sir. I don't think he is important enough.' Years later Wylie remarked 'I told the truth, but my God, I was far off the mark.'

He returned to private practice after the court-martials. Wylie again took up work on behalf of the government in 1919, this time as law advisor under

Lord French. This period saw the escalation of the War of Independence. It was also the era of the Black and Tans, ambushes and reprisals.

It was a difficult time for Wylie, who was a liberal Unionist but a fair-minded and honest man. He had come to realise that a certain measure of independence needed to be granted to Ireland. He spoke out against the Black and Tans and the policy of official reprisals. He acted as an advisor and as a conduit between the Lloyd George government and the Irish Republican leaders.

In August 1920, Wylie had become prominent in a conciliation policy backed by General Macready and several others in the Dublin Castle administration including Andrew Cope. At this time, Lloyd George was bent on introducing a coercion measure. The Law and Order Bill. This bill would not be accompanied by any substantive permanent policy and in Wylie's own words, would not coerce but would aggravate and settle nothing. Military coercion was repellent to his mind so he resigned from office. Later that year he was appointed as a high court judge.

Following the Treaty and the formation of the Irish Free State Wylie received the seal of office for the second time as a senior judge. This time on the advice of the Executive Council of Saorstát Éireann. He held this position along with his job as Judicial Commissioner of the Irish Land Commission until 1936. He was a most influential person and his advice was eagerly sought and acted on by many interests in the emerging new state. Through his association with the Royal Dublin Society, he assisted in the transfer of the society's Leinster House to the new state as a parliament house.

As a keen horseman, he devoted much time to equestrian sports. He served as a steward of the Irish Turf Club and the national Hunt Steeplechase Committee. He was hugely involved in enhancing the international prestige of the Dublin Horse Show and Lord Holmpatrick his near neighbour, and Capt. F. Baron assisted him. He also was involved in advising in the setting up of the Irish army's Equitation School in McKee Barracks.

Wylie was one of the first members of the Society and General Council of the Irish Red Cross and served on it with Áine Ceannt, widow of Eamonn Ceannt, whom he prosecuted in 1916. In fact, Ceannt's brother later became

Wylie's registrar in the Land Commission. Helena Moloney of Cumann na mBan also served with Wylie on the Red Cross committee. No bitterness was ever shown between any of these people.

In all his dealings with the various historic figures of the time he possibly disagreed more with Éamon de Valera over many aspects of policy than any other, however, in the twilight of his years it was 'Dev' who telephoned him several times with good wishes and appreciation of his great work for Ireland.

Only one personality of the time seems to attract negative comment from Wylie's pen – in an uncharacteristic comment he remarks that having made a fool of himself on the Boundary Commission negotiations, Eoin MacNeill remained in the comparative obscurity for which he was admirably suited.

In latter years, Judge Wylie continued to pursue his interest in bloodstock and the lands and the lanes around Clonsilla House echoed to the sounds of galloping hooves. Ill health in his eighties forced him to sell Clonsilla House and move into the Stephen's Green club and he died in 1964 at the age of 83 and is buried in Clonsilla graveyard beside his beloved wife Ida, close to the site of the former Clonsilla House, now the modern housing estate of Portersgate.

Clonsilla House was destroyed by fire in the 1970s and all that remains of the estate is a house on an island of land at the front of St Mary's church in Clonsilla. This mock Tudor style building was built in 1901 as a farriers forge for the Clonsilla House estate and stud. The then owner's name was William Edward Humphrey Steed and it is his initials that appear on a plaque on the side of the house. So there is the answer to the puzzle for all those passers-by who wondered what the letters meant.

ONGAR HOUSE

Ongar House was originally called Hansfield House. The Hon. Hans Blackwood owned the house and surrounding lands, hence the name.

Thomas Williams owned the house in the mid 1800s, followed by Patrick Bobbett who was descended from a French mariner. The family later conducted a thriving market garden business in Dublin for years. Patrick's son William Bobbett inherited Hansfield in 1886.

In 1926, the new owner Col Arthur Pollock arrived and some years later changed the name to Ongar House after a town in England. The Aga Khan purchased the property in 1943 and his son Prince Ali Khan managed the stud. His wife, the film star, Rita Hayworth turned many a head on her many visits to Ongar. Prince Ali Khan died in a motor accident in France.

American businessman Donal Strahlem purchased the property, and on his death Phil Sweeney, a Mayo man, bought the house and kept it until 1989. The stud farm was then sold on to a subsidiary of Monarch Properties who sold it to Manor Park Homebuilders in 1995.

The imposing Georgian mansion now dominates the fine square in the new Ongar Village. This village is an architectural gem and the developers must be congratulated on creating such a picturesque traditional Irish village in the midst of their large housing development.

4

PORTERSTOWN, COOLMINE, CORDUFF AND MULHUDDART

The church of St Mochta's, Porterstown, was built on land given by the Warren family. Work on the building commenced in 1890. William Hague, FRIA, was the Architect involved and John Dooley the Clerk of Works. Archbishop Walsh laid the foundation stone, assisted by Very Rev. M. Donovan, PP, Blanchardstown, and Rev. Jas. Williams, CC, Porterstown. A parishioner named Wilson gave £500 towards the building fund while a Mr William Bobbett, who was joint treasurer, donated £100. The archbishop contributed £500. The total budget was £2,000. The building replaced the old chapel beside Porterstown National School, which was later the Scouts Den.

Porterstown High School – or the National School, to give it its correct name – because of its dimensions and curious appearance has been the subject of many legends. The truth is more prosaic, however. James Kennedy, a licensed vintner with a business in Capel Street, built it in 1853. He and his brother Charles, who lived locally, contributed a suit of clothes to every boy with 100 days' attendance. There is an earlier reference in this work refuting some of the legends relating to the school. There was acrimony between Fr Dungan, PP, Blanchardstown, and Rev. Sadlier, rector of Castleknock, however concerning the religious teaching of children. A tart reference to RCs and bibles made by Lord Eglington, the lord lieutenant, on a visit to the school did nothing to heal this rift. There were allegations of proselytising and rows about staff. Both men of the cloth were highly thought of by their respective congregations and were good people. A sign of the times was the fact that religion often got in the way of Christianity, and to be fair both men were acting from deeply ingrained and dearly held principles.

It was not until January 1965 that both Protestant and Catholic joined in common public prayer, at a service in the parish field conducted by Canon Neil, Church of Ireland parish of Castleknock, and Canon Crowe, Roman Catholic parish of Blanchardstown. This was the first ecumenical service in the area. The school, which is reputed to be haunted, closed down in 1963.

ALONG THE BANKS OF THE ROYAL CANAL

Close to Porterstown National School is the 'deep sinking' of the Royal Canal. It lies between Kennan Bridge and Carhampton Bridge (also known Callaghan's Bridge) and was the scene of a dreadful tragedy on 25 November 1845. Sixteen people were drowned when a barge struck a projection from the bank at McGoverns rocks. In the ensuing panic, the movement of passengers trying to escape further destabilised the barge, causing the disaster. Most of the dead were from Longford and Mullingar. It appeared from the coroner's examination that a free passenger named Teeling was allowed by Capt. O'Connor of Longford to steer the boat but that he was inebriated and hit the bank. The jury

The Royal Canal from Kennan Bridge
Photograph by Fr Eugene Kennedy

Kellystown Spring Well on the Royal Canal
bank. Alas, now a trickle, owing to building
development in the area
Photograph by Fr Eugene Kennedy

also implicated the normal steersman James Dunne. Blame was apportioned to all three men. Local tradition asserts that eerie sounds emanate from the location of the accident on the anniversary of the event.

Fr Michael Dungan, PP, Blanchardstown, when alerted of the tragedy, galloped through the dark November night on horseback along the narrow lanes and canal towpath to perform the last rites. One of the passengers, Private Jessop of the Eighth Hussars, was conspicuous in his efforts to save lives and was praised in the newspapers of the day. It is not widely known that these boats were capable of speeds of eight or nine miles per hour, allowing for times spent at locks, and were faster and more comfortable than coach travel on bad roads. In 1846, however, construction work on the new railway began and passenger travel on the canals greatly declined. My own father told me that his grandfather used to reminisce about picking blackberries on the canal banks while this new railway was being laid down. Incidentally, the work provided by this project helped greatly in reducing the effects of the Great Famine in the locality.

Carhampton Bridge was renamed Callaghan's Bridge, after a popular local landowner. Due to the excesses carried out by Lord Carhampton in putting down the 1798 Rising, the local people removed his name from the bridge. A pleasant walk along the Royal Canal bank from Kirkpatrick Bridge towards Kennan Bridge leads to what remains of the Kellystown spring well. This well was discovered during the construction of the Royal Canal; the waters diverted beneath the tow path through two arches to empty into the canal. The well was an extremely valuable discovery in 1795, when piped water outside Dublin city was a rarity. This beautiful well surrounded by ferns and wildflowers is now less than a trickle, building developments nearby appear to have altered the flow. Fine purple marl suitable for staining paper was also discovered on land owned by the Troys adjoining the canal.

Work on the canal commenced in 1790 and it took sixteen years to reach Mullingar. The delay was partly caused by the need to blast through the hard calcareous limestone of Carpenterstown. This stretch is known as the 'deep sinking', and is over two miles long, almost twenty-eight feet deep in parts and cost

Drawing of Mulhuddart Church by Gabriel de Branger, 1775
Courtesy of Fingal County Council

more than £40,000. (To illustrate how expensive this was at the time, we should note that Alexander Kirkpatrick, who gave his name to the canal bridge, bought 532 acres of land at Coolmine, including villages, for £14,000). This massive cost bankrupted the project, and the Royal Canal was never a commercial success. The canal should have been routed further north, but the duke of Leinster is reported to have wanted it to pass his estate at Carton, and the Kennan family, who also had Kennan Bridge named after them, wanted it to pass their estate. The Kennans lived in Annefield House, where Archbishop Troy was born. They were in the ironmongery business and supplied most of the railings and iron-work for Phoenix Park. Kirkpatrick Bridge was named after a local landowner of whom more later.

A brief look at the Royal Canal is worthwhile because it is one of the major physical features of the locality. The Royal Canal scheme was proposed by John Binns, a former director of the Grand Canal, who fell out with his directors and thus set up the rival canal. The cause of the row, Long John Binns – or The Devil's Darning Needle, as he was called – had made his money from his many footwear factories. Apparently, someone on the board had referred to him as a cobbler. The source of supply for the water is largely Lough Owel near Mullingar. There are forty-seven locks and there were originally eighty-six bridges, most of which were in near perfect condition 200 years later. Construction commenced in May 1790 at Cross Guns Bridge and went westwards and eastwards from there. Two thousand men were employed in gangs of 140. Wages were originally 5p (10d) a day, which increased to 9p (1s 6d) a day for labourers after a strike. By 1792, the canal had encountered problems at Carpenterstown. It was originally estimated by Richard Evans, the engineer responsible, that it would cost £10,223 to cut a route through nearly two miles of rock. It eventually cost almost £42,000 which was a huge sum at that time. The canal should have taken a more northerly direction for two reasons: such a route would have been easier both geologically and topographically, and the chosen route was too close to the newly built Grand Canal and would be competing for the same business. The duke of Leinster – rather than the engineers – got his way, however.

This route involved building a one hundred foot aqueduct across the River Rye Water at Leixlip. Evans again underestimated, by almost £8,500; it eventually cost £28,230, and by 1794, the company was bankrupted. The levels were incorrect, some lock chambers were badly designed and the poor-quality timber used in the lock gates was starting to rot. At this stage, just over fifteen miles of canal had been completed. By means of borrowing from banks, issuing stock and raising money from parliament, it was eventually completed in 1817 by the engineer John Killally. It had cost £1,422,000 – about €120 million in today's terms. The barges, pulled along by horses on the towpath, carried grain, potatoes, vegetables and building materials, but the main cargo was turf, won from the midland bogs. Passengers, who travelled first- or second-class, were not permitted to smoke. Dogs and servants went second-class.

The Midland Great Western Railway Company purchased the canal in 1845 with the intention of draining it and running the railway along its bed and under the bridges. This scheme would have used the existing works for the canal effectively and cheaply. Although the railway company spent £318,860 acquiring the canal, the project was not allowed, for legal reasons and instead we have the lovely linear park that is the Royal Canal today. The railway eventually killed off canal trade; the last barge ceased working the canal in July

1955. The last complete voyage of a working barge on the canal was made by the *Lark*.

Since 1974, the Royal Canal Amenity Group has carried out Trojan work, and the canal is again navigable from Blanchardstown to Mullingar. It is managed by the Board of Works, which hopes within the next few years to reopen the whole canal, right to the Shannon.

The engineer responsible for the Midland and Great Western Railway was George Hemans, son of the poetess Felicia Dorotha Hemans. She wrote the poem 'Casablanca' which begins with the verse 'The boy stood on the burning deck ...'

COOLMINE

Coolmine (Cúil Mhín – 'the smooth-backed hill), the old site of St Mochta's first chapel, changed hands over the centuries, and parts of it were owned at various times by Luttrells, Dillons, Eagers, Boltons, Rooneys, Dalys and Russells. The Down Survey of 1655 states that 'Sir Edward Bolton, English Protestant' held the lands of Coolmine and Ringwellstowns which consisted of 420 acres and a thatched house with two stone chimneys, a barn, a stable and several little cottages. Bolton, who was chief baron of the exchequer, acquired the estate for the earl of Thomond, who in turn had it from one Walter Peppard, who previously gained ownership of it following the dissolution of St Mary's abbey. In 1780 Alexander Kirkpatrick of Drumcondra House and formerly of Scotland bought the estate from the Bolton family.

The Kirkpatrick family motto is 'I make sure' and their emblem is a dagger. One of their ancestors made sure with his dagger, that the king, Robert Bruce of Scotland, was safe from an intended assassin – hence the emblem and the motto. The Kirkpatrick family in the Scottish line became connected with the Bonaparte family through a daughter who married Count de Monitijo; she in turn was the mother of Empress Eugenie, wife of Napoleon III. Alexander Kirkpatrick was a director of the Royal Canal Company; the bridge at Carpenterstown is named for him. The Kirkpatrick family sold their land in Coolmine about 1925 to John Evans of County Wicklow. Dudley Douglas Kirkpatrick lodged with Miss Sadie Ellis until the 1940s in Woodview House. Another branch of the family settled near Celbridge. A member of this side of the family who worked in the British Foreign Office before the Second World War was called on to identify Hitler's deputy, Rudolf Hess, following his flight to Scotland in May 1941. Coolmine Community School and Coolmine Therapeutic Community now occupy these lands.

The Segrave family also lived in the Coolmine area. The history of this distinguished family, whose principal seat was in Cabra, is given in a later chapter.

During the 1850s, human skeletons were unearthed at Coolmine by farm workers; the skeletons were reckoned to date back to the period of the ancient priory and were reinterred after examination. In 1798, a terrible conflagration broke out in the home of Nicholas Eager of Coolmine, and the house was destroyed, leaving four children and their widowed father without a roof over their head. The fire started in an oven in which bread was being baked. The Eager family later lived in Abbey Cottage. A description of Clonsilla in 1890 says: 'There is nothing worthy of the name of a village or hamlet. The railway station alone has preserved it from oblivion.' I don't accept the description then and I know it is not true today – oblivion how are you!

The old signal box at Clonsilla is a well-known landmark. It was burned during the 'Troubles', restored later and is a fine example of early railway architecture.

DARBY'S HILL WELL

Near Blanchardstown, in the vicinity of the rear of the Tractamotors garage, a holy well existed. This area was known as Darby's Hill. If you wished to be cured, you visited the well, dipped a rag in the water and hung it on a nearby whitethorn bush. As the rag disintegrated and gradually disappeared, so did the ailment. This well required nine visits for a cure to take place. This passage of time generally meant that minor illnesses were cured because of the old medical adage: 'Treat a cold and it will last two weeks, don't and it will last a fortnight.'

Porterstown National School
Photograph by Fr Eugene Kennedy

If this did not work, the patient was probably not around to make a tenth visit to deny the efficacy of the cure. There are many holy wells throughout the world; they are mostly pre-Christian in origin. This part of County Dublin is particularly favoured with holy wells – Mulhuddart, Diswellstown, Castleknock, Lucan and Caeveen being the better-known locations of them. There is also a beautiful sweet water well on the Lower Road in the direction of the Strawberry Beds known only to a few – and I am keeping the secret!

CORDUFF

Corduff (Corr Dhubh, 'the dark hill') was the seat of the Warren family, Norman settlers who also gave their name to Warrenstown, County Meath. They originally lived in the Swords area and one branch of the family settled in County Kildare. The de la Felde family originally settled in Corduff, during the time Richard Tyrell fourth baron of Castleknock, controlled the barony. The de la Feldes sent a mounted archer to a great hosting at Tara during the reign of Elizabeth I.

As we have seen, according to the Down Survey of 1655, 'Coolduffe (Corduff) is the property of Will Warren Irish Papist and comprises 143 acres and includes a stone house slated, one barn and stable thatched, several cottages, a small orchard and garden.'

Will Warren also held 232 acres of the Castletown part of Castleknock in mortgage. The de la Feldes seem to have had the estate forfeited to the crown for political or religious reasons. The Warrens subsequently had their Corduff lands forfeited for a time, when a man called Nolan farmed them. There was a bit of chicanery even in those days, however: one William Culliford of his majesty's revenue was charged with seizing the land to his private advantage.

BONNIE PRINCE CHARLIE

Following the Williamite confiscations, the Warren family moved to France. Richard Warren joined the French army and later Rothe's Irish Regiment, where he rose to the rank of colonel. He was involved in efforts to re-establish the exiled house of Stuart as the true line of succession and arranged with shipowner friends of his in Nantes called Walsh – who were originally from Kilkenny and in whose ship James II had escaped to France after the Boyne – to provide a brigantine of 110 tons and 18 guns to bring his grandson, Prince Charles Edward Stuart (Bonnie Prince Charlie), to Scotland. At first the Scots were slow to rally to his standard but following several Jacobite victories the rising gained momentum.

Warren joined the prince in Scotland as aide-de-camp to Lord John Murray, commander-in-chief of the Scottish army, with the rank of colonel. The Jacobite army advanced until it reached Derby. The Stuart supporters in England failed to rally to the standard and Bonnie Prince Charlie withdrew his army to Scotland. This army had been within a couple of days march of London, and had he stayed the French would have mustered all the Irish regiments in France for him rather then the token number of Irish soldiers previously sent.

Charles' brother Henry had been gathering a force of 10,000 to add to the original army. London would have fallen – and history been rewritten – if things had worked out. With the retreat, morale fell and bickering occurred between the leaders. Warren returned to France to negotiate extra aid. He met Louis XV, who made him a knight of St Louis and ordered two ships loaded with provisions to set sail for Scotland.

While Warren was recruiting men and gathering funds William, duke of Cumberland, with a well-trained army outnumbering the largely untrained Jacobite army by two to one and having arms and equipment of the most up-to-date kind, annihilated the clansmen and their Irish auxiliaries at Culloden Moor near Inverness. In fact, the seasoned Irish soldiers saved the prince's life that day. The battle lasted forty-five minutes, and the round-up that followed saw butchery beyond belief. To this day, the duke of Cumberland has two plants named for him: in England a flower called 'Sweet William' and in Scotland a weed called 'Stinking Billy.' The prince was a hunted refugee for five months; he even had to dress up as a servant woman until rescued by Col Warren.

On his return to France, the Old Pretender, James III, awarded Warren a baronetcy. Warren had a long army career after this and was raised to the rank of brigadier-general following a secret mission to London in 1750. He became governor of Belle Isle off the coast of Brittany and died there in June 1775, aged seventy-five. The portrait of Monsieur Richard Augustus Warren, baron of Corduff, chevalier baronet of Great Britain, chevalier of the Royal and Military Order of St Louis, field marshal and commandant of Belle Isle today hangs on the wall of a Second World War German bunker that has been converted into a local museum near Quiberon in Brittany. The writer discovered this fact coincidentally while on holiday in the region. Had he a camera? Yes, but no film so the portrait will have to wait.

The Warren family also owned the area now occupied by Castleknock College and part of the lands near White's Gate. Their lands at Corduff later became the property of the Egan family.

According to the 1930 Post Office Directory, Miss B. Murphy lived at Courtduff and A.G. Ringroom at Corduff. The road from Corduff to Cloghran through Ballycoolin was an area of rebel activity during the War of Independence; subsequently the Blanchardstown volunteers took the republican side in the Civil War. The Farnan family who lived in this area gave their all in the fight for Irish freedom. In a later chapter we will dwell on the 1916–1923 period and what it meant locally.

THE MARE AND THE FOAL

On the right-hand side of the road, at the junction with Ratoath Road, there is a quarry with an old burial ground at the rear. Across the road, behind Dolly's public house, is the townland of Godamendy. The legend goes that, during the penal times, a priest was saying Mass in the ruins of Cloghranhidred, a very early Christian place of worship. During the most solemn part of the Mass, a parishioner came up to the priest and whispered into his ear that his mare and foal had been stolen. 'Well, God amend ye!' said the priest. Immediately across the fields at the edge of what is now the quarry the mare and foal were rooted to the spot and the thief apprehended; the townland was thereafter called Godamendy. The marks of the hooves of the mare and foal can be seen to this day etched in rock, and the area is still known as the 'Mare and Foal.' I walked the quarry with my father in 1978. He was then in his seventies, but could not locate the marks. He related this story as being handed down for generations. The marks in the rock (they could be clearly seen in times gone by) were fossilised prints. The townland appears to have been known as Godamendy from before penal times, but it is a wonderful story.

At the time of the Norman invasion, All Saints priory owned these lands. By 1655, as the Down Survey indicates, they had become the property of City of Dublin, and reference is made to the wall of an old castle. This was probably the ruin of the old church. In the early 1970s, massive house-building occurred in the Corduff area, a new parish was created in 1976, and a new parish church St Patrick's was consecrated in 1980. The area of Ballycoolin up to Cloghran is now a fine industrial estate, providing employment for thousands in the locality. Nearby between Corduff and Buzzardstown (Bossards after a family of that name) are the imposing buildings of Blanchardstown Institute of Technology opened in 1999 and presently catering for 1,500 students.

MULHUDDART

Mulhuddart, once a small hamlet, is now a vast built-up area. The earliest records show Richard Porter of Porterstown making a bequest to the church in Mulhuddart in 1472. The name Mulhuddart appears to mean 'the mound of Cuthbert.' This saint was born in Northumbria in 634 and, although steeped in the Celtic traditions of the church, accepted and indeed promulgated the Roman reforms of the Synod of Whitby. He was inclined to the hermetical life and died in March 687. He was buried at Lindisfarne, where he was Prior. During the Viking attacks of 998, his body was moved to Durham Cathedral, where it became an object of veneration, with a pilgrimage to it on 20 March each year. He is also associated with Kilmahuddrick ('church of Cuthbert'), an area outside Clondalkin.

Another source gives the name as Maolaedard (Mulladh Eadrad, 'the high place of the sun's fire'). Standing on the hill on a summer's evening watching the setting sun, one can see how that name could be ascribed to it. Or it may be 'bald Aedh's (Hugh's) height.' Aedh Mac Morna killed Finn MacCumhail's father at the Battle of Castleknock (Cnucha) and was thereafter known as Goll MacMorna, having lost an eye in the encounter. Take your pick – the last is my own choice.

The well, now known as Lady's Well, was originally dedicated to Cuthbert and appears to have been rededicated to the Virgin Mary in or about 1300. Richard Belling, secretary to the Supreme Council of the Confederation of Kilkenny, who brought the militant Archbishop Rinuccini (d.1665) to Ireland, is buried here, or, as the *Dublin University Magazine* of October 1853 says with the minimum bias, 'His ashes repose in the country which he spent his life inflaming.'

In September 1690 a company of Williamite soldiers under Col Foulkes sheltered in the church from the rain while en route to Dublin and were slain, apparently in cold blood to the last man. Pat Moore, John Cummin, Phil Strong and Andrew Cannon were executed in Thomas Street for this act.

PORTER'S GUIDE AND DIRECTORY FOR MULHUDDART (AND CLOGHRAN) 1912

Mulhuddart is a small village about a mile and a half from Blanchardstown with a population of about 120, in a purely agricultural district. There is a Post Office, and a National School under the capable control of Mr McDonnell.

Mulhuddart Post Office: Mrs Carroll, Postmistress.

Mulhuddart National School: Mr Michael McDonnell, Principal: Miss Carr, Workmistress. Average attendance 50.

MULHUDDART RESIDENTS

(B) Bermingham, Patrick, Huntstown House, Dairyman. (C) Carr, Bros., Grocers and Spirit Merchants. Carr, F. Moortown. Carr, Michael, Blakestown. Carr, Wm, Parslickstown. Carroll, James, Builder and Contractor. Carthy, P. Blakestown. (D) Donegan, Patrick, Cruicerath. Doyle, Gerald, Belgree. (F) Fitzsimins, T. Damestown. Flynn, J. Littlepace. (G) Graham, Miss, Larch Grove. Greaven, Mr Blakestown. Goodwin, P. and Sons, Harness and Saddle Makers. (H) Hartford, John, Buzzardstown. Hoey, Ms, Buzzardstown. Hoey, W.G., Mountain View. Hughes, Richard, Tolka Cottage. (K) Kearns, Mrs, Ballycoolan. (L) Lacy, Thos., Smith and Farrier. Leckin, Miss, Whitestown. (M) McCracken, Thomas, Kilmartin. Mulhuddart Church, Rev. C.W. O'Hara, M.A., Incumbent, The Rectory. (P) Philips, R. Belgree. (S) Seagrave, James, Rosetown. Smyth, J. Pacefield. Smyth, John, Damestown. Sub-Post Office – Miss M. Carroll, Postmistress. (W) Weldon, The Dowager Lady, Tyrellstown House. Wilkinson, R. Cattle Salesman, Powerstown, and 41, Prussia Street. Willan, John Hone, J.P., Kilmartin House. White, Nicholas, Belgree.

CLOGHRAN RESIDENTS

(D) Daly, Thomas, Rosemount. Dodd, Christopher, Castlemoate. Donovan, Robt, Little Forest. (H) Hayden, James, Redmoortown. Howison, Richard, Cloghran House.

LADY'S WELL

The well's day of pilgrimage was 8 September, the Feast of the Nativity of the Blessed Virgin, and thousands flocked to it. More attended for the *uisce beatha* than the *fíor uisce coisreacain* ('holy water') and there were scenes of drunkenness and riotous behaviour among the tents and drinking booths set up for the occasion. Eventually the church, with the assistance of the civil authority, stopped this *patrún* or 'pattern'. I quote *Faulkner's Dublin Journal* of 15 August 1754:

> We are assured that the Roman Catholic clergy to prevent as far as in them lieth, the enormities and scandalous excesses that are annually committed at the Well near Malaedard, commonly called Lady's Well, have prevailed on the landholders contiguous thereto not to permit any tents or booths to be erected hereafter upon any part of their lands; of which it is judged proper to give notice in this public manner, to prevent a disappointment to such publicans as usually erected tents or booths near said well.

It was reputed that the well had nine cures.

The graveyard was one of the few close to the city where Roman Catholic clergy were allowed officiate at funerals during penal times – hence the many tombstones raised to people from the city.

There is a tradition that the well was originally on the same side of the road as the graveyard, and that someone in authority tried to fill it in and it sprung up in its present location. The nearby townlands of Cruiserath, Tyrellstown, Buzzardstown (Bossardstown) and Huntstown take their names from Norman invaders. Damastown appears to come from Our Lady (Notre Dame), referring to the well. One Nicholas Hunt of Huntstown was outlawed by the government for treason during the late 1300s. During the Famine a local farmer, Mr Carr of Parslickstown House, sowed turnip seed instead of potatoes and was thus able to provide sustenance for his neighbours, as turnips are not affected by potato blight.

Lady's Well Mulhuddart
Courtesy of Fingal County Council

The members of this family became great supporters of Parnell, who lunched in their home at Parslickstown when he stopped off en route to his Meath constituency.

A local legend related by Peter Sobolewski in his and Donal MacPolin's book *Blanchardstown, Castleknock and the Park twixt Liffey and Tolka* tell of an incident in England that resulted in the acquisition of the Carrs 164 acre farm.

A man was being publicly executed somewhere in England and the state hangman offered him the chance to say his last words. In a strong voice the condemned man enquired 'is there any among you from Mulhuddart?' Surprisingly so, there was, and the condemned man told him go to Blair's well and you will find there a crock of gold. The man returned to Blanchardstown, located the gold and used this to purchase Parslickstown in 1840.

Parslickstown was the property of a John Dowdall who also owned the adjoining Macetown in the mid 1300s. This became the property of Thomasine Talbot in the 1500s, later becoming the aforementioned Richard Belling's property along with Tyrellstown and Buzzardstown.

On the corner of Church is a hostelry once owned by the Donnelly family and called the 'Shanty', where generations of north Dublin families dropped in for refreshments after a funeral. Bertie Donnelly was a famous racing cyclist and, with another local, Herbie Breedon, dominated this sport for years. Frank Baird completed this cycling trio, which did so much for a sport that was then in its infancy. Cycling as a sport had a huge following in the locality at that time.

The Church of Ireland parish of Mulhuddart built a beautiful small church near Hollywood Rath in 1870–71. It was consecrated by Archbishop Richard Chevnix Trench (a relative of Lord Ashtown and Rev. Sadlier) on 19 December 1871 and was dedicated to Saint Thomas the Apostle; coincidentally the Roman Catholic church in Laurel Lodge is dedicated to the same saint. Another apostle is commemorated in the name of St Luke the Evangelist – the new Roman Catholic church built in Mulhuddart after the parish was constituted from Blanchardstown in 1993.

5

BLANCHARDSTOWN

Blanchardstown is and has for many years been a much busier, bigger, more commercial and more populous village than any other one in the area. The name is taken from the Blanchard family, who were granted their estate possibly from the fourth baron Tyrell in about 1250–60. There was a further landlord-tenant relationship between the two families in County Tipperary. The name 'Blanchard' appears to refer to white hair or fair hair, from the Norman French blanch, meaning 'white.' (We use the word in, among other ways, a culinary sense today, e.g. to blanch vegetables). The name 'Plunkett' (Blanchette) has a similar origin. It may also have referred to a tendency to turn white in battle. The name was in the area for many years, but apart from giving their name to the village the family did nothing of note, good or bad; if they had, they would appear in the old records. The name Villa Blanchard is used in the documents of the time.

In the early 1900s the name Baile Luindín was given as the Irish name for Blanchardstown. A signpost on the Navan Road at Mooney's Cross proclaimed to all and sundry that Blanchardstown – Baile Luindín, lay three miles distant. To find out how the name Baile Luindín came about we have to look at the arduous task Seosamh Laoide was delegated by Conradh na Gaeilge, of collecting the Irish name for every town and village in Ireland where a post office existed.

Not every town has an Irish name as most towns only came into being after the Anglo-Norman invasion and in the area of the Pale, English was largely the vernacular from the fourteenth century onwards.

From conversations with his mother, Seosamh learned that on her way by coach to Dublin along the Navan Road, the last stage where horses were changed was Baile Luindin. Seosamh put two and two together and calculated that it must be Blanchardstown and thus Blanchardstown became Baile Luindin. However, this was a case of two plus two making five as Baile Luindín is Blundellstown, County Meath, near Tara of the high kings.

However, Baile Luindín remained from 1905 until the late 1980s when the mistake was somewhat reluctantly admitted and the Norman-French name Blanchard was Gaelicised into the awful non-meaning Bhlainséir, as in Baile Bhlainséir. What would be wrong with Baile Blanchard – a more direct translation?

In the United States there is a town of Blanchard which is now a suburb of Oklahoma City. There are also towns called Blanchard in Louisiana, Idaho and North Dakota. Incidentially, locals always pronounced the name Blancherstown and not Blanchardstown – however, sin scéal eile.

In 1351, John Owen acquired Diswellstown after one of the Deuswell family fell out of favour and was attainted. Owen also acquired Blanchardstown at this time. In about 1450 a Blanchardstown character called Phillip Cowherd, styling himself as Phillip Mounsell, forged deeds relating to land in Castleknock and sold them on, in a form of medieval conmanship. He was caught and parliament was called to cancel the forgeries.

In 1655 'Robert Dillon, Irish Papist, owned 190 acres of Blanchardstown and Simon Luttrell, Irish Papist, 10 acres and Christopher Barnwell 7 acres.' There were two thatched houses, a barn, another little cottage, a young orchard and garden and a mill on the estate. The member of parliament representing Newcastle, William Rowles, lived in Blanchardstown in the early 1600s, followed by his son Henry and grandson Richard Ball.

The most prominent resident at that time was Richard Bereford, who died in 1662. In his will he left books and a bass violin, a watch, a great deal of plate, his bay nag, his white nag and some livestock. He wanted to be buried in Ratoath and left the people of that village his brewing pan, which he had there. At that time there were only thirty-one people living in Blanchardstown. Much of present-day Blanchardstown was covered by the Great Scaldwood, which was home to wolves and, further back, wild boar.

THE GREAT SCALDWOOD

This relic of Ireland's ancient forest stretched from the River Tolka (meaning 'flood') beyond Coolmine and was inhabited by wolves up till at least 1652. In that year a wolf cull was ordered by the authorities, as these predators were threatening livestock. The wars and rebellions of those years brought about a reduction in hunting animals and an increase in the hunting of human quarry. The wolves grew in numbers and thus became a menace. Wolves preyed mainly on livestock and rarely attacked humans. The last remaining wolf in Ireland was killed near Baltinglass, County Wicklow, by John Watson in 1786.

During this time it is believed that Ireland, had a slightly warmer climate than it does now, it was much more heavily forested that at present. It is estimated that for every million trees planted, the average temperature increases by one degree Fahrenheit. The wholesale destruction of the Irish forests largely to provide charcoal and timber for the Royal Navy caused climatic and pastoral changes of huge importance. Ireland was famous for its oak trees and Irish oak was widely used in the Palace of Westminster. An excellent example of the use of Irish timber is the roof of Dunsoghly Castle near St Margaret's, County Dublin.

According to the Hearth Tax, the following surnames appear in Blanchardstown rolls: Dempsey, Cosgrove, Lowth, Plunkett, Skully, Boylan, Callan, Jordan, Georges and Bamber. The death on the gallows in 1783 of a local woman, Bridget Segrave is recorded in the *Freeman's Journal*. She was convicted of arson for allegedly burning down a house belonging to a Mr Morgan. Until her dying breath she protested her innocence. Was the owner of the house the Richard Morgan who left instructions in his will on his death in 1784 for the building of Morgan's school on the Navan road? Was Bridget a member of the Coolmine, Cabra or Finglas Segraves? Was she jilted by Morgan? Did she do it at all? The veil of time shrouds the truth from us.

CHURCHES AND CLERICS

The churches in Castleknock and Clonsilla were used by the people of Blanchardstown until the time of the Reformation, Blanchardstown not being a large enough entity in itself to have its own parish church. In 1537 Henry VIII's 'reforms' were introduced by the Irish parliament. At that time, it would appear, Rev. Travers was the incumbent in Castleknock; Rev. John Fyche held the vicarage in 1474 and was principal official of the Dublin consistorial court and was succeeded by Rev. Meagh. Sir John Dongan was vicar in 1540; he was followed by Rev. John Rice in 1615.

This period was confusing from a religious point of view as Henry's 1533 changes were minor and the religious policies of his son Edward VI (1547–53), being more Protestant in nature, were suddenly overturned by his successor, Mary Tudor (1553–58), who restored Roman Catholicism. When Elizabeth I came to power, in 1558, the Church of Ireland and Protestantism were re-established.

It is hard to imagine in today's secular society the effect these changes and counter changes had on the faithful, not to mention on clergy and ecclesiastics, who had temporal reasons – their salaries – as well as spiritual ones to wrestle with their consciences. Years afterwards, Jonathan Swift, in his book *Gullivers Travels* (1726), satirised these events in the story of the Lilliputians going to war over which end the egg should be topped before eaten.

In 1630 the Rev. Harris, chaplain to the Luttrells, and a Rev. Patrick Gargan used to say Mass mostly in the private houses of the gentry. Later on, Mass was said in ruined Celtic churches or Mass rocks. There is a tradition of a Mass rock situated on Lower Road and another in Cloghran. In the latter part of the century Rev. Walter Cruce, DD, who was ordained in 1692, was parish priest of Mulhuddart, Castleknock, Clonsilla, Cloghran, and Chapelizod. He held the position of archdeacon and was probably one of the family that gave its name to Cruiserath. Rev. Oliver Doyle was parish priest of Castleknock in 1704. In the same year Rev. Francis Delamer was parish priest of Clonsilla and Rev. Manus Quigley was parish priest of Chapelizod. Fr Quigley was ordained in 1679 in Louth by St Oliver Plunkett.

St Brigid's church, Blanchardstown
Photograph by Brendan Campion

On 29 October 1837 Mass was celebrated by Fr Michael Dungan in the new church of St Brigid's, Blanchardstown, which was then unfinished. This being a time of great poverty, twenty-six years passed before the work was completed. The beautiful spire was erected in 1858 by Beardwood & Son and is of Flemish design, and it is thought that Fr Joseph Joy Dean who was in the parish from 1802 to 1836 (as parish priest in his last 11 years) got the idea from his time on the continent. Fr Dean was a first cousin of Henry Joy McCracken, the leader of the rebellion in Antrim in 1798.

A Fr Myles McPharlan was appointed parish priest in 1803. Before that Fr Myles McPharlan was a curate, attached to St Mary's chapel in Liffey Street when he was much discomfited to learn that his humble apartment featured in the billeting arrangements of a milita unit brought over to suppress the 1798 Rebellion. Major John Traubman, commander of the Manx Fencibles, was to be his compulsory lodger. The Penal Laws, though largely relaxed, were still on the statute books and it was prudent for Catholic clergy to 'put up and shut up.' In spite of this, the major and himself became friends until the Major's return to the Isle of Man.

Five years later Fr Myles was promoted as parish priest of Blanchardstown. His new church was little more than a cabin similar but larger to those in which his impoverished flock dwelt. It was located a few yards to the northeast of the present St Brigid's church in Blanchardstown. Poverty in the area was endemic.

Fr Myles proposed the idea of establishing a brick-making factory to provide employment in the locality. His many talents did not include good business sense; consequently the venture failed leaving many disgruntled creditors. His 'cloth', far from encouraging his creditors to extend a degree of latitude, presented an ideal opportunity for some to deny such latitude.

Back then debtors were imprisoned until the debt was discharged. Debtors' prisons were far from congenial, with a high mortality rate amongst the inmates. Therefore, Fr Myles hastily decamped to the relative safety of the Isle of Man.

There he renewed his friendship with Major Traubman, now an influential member of the House of Keys – the Manx parliament, and a substantial landowner. Part of the lands owned by the major included the ruins of St Brigid's convent, a pre-Reformation nunnery. According to local tradition it was founded by St Brigid who is reputed to have died there.

The major donated the site to Fr Myles, where he built a church dedicating it to St Brigid, the patron saint of his Blanchardstown church and co-incidentally of the old convent. This was the first Catholic church built on the island since the Reformation. The census of 1791 listed only 25 Catholic residents on the islands who were served on an occasional basis by a priest travelling over by boat from Dublin. Nowadays a thriving Roman Catholic community exists in the Isle of Man. A stone tablet in the fine St Mary's church in Douglas is inscribed:

> To God's Greatest and Best
> Rev. Miles McPharlan
> A Parish Priest near Dublin
> Restored to its ancient worship
> The Chapel of St Bridget
> In the year 1814.

Archbishop Murray summoned him back to Dublin in 1825. On failing to appear, Blanchardstown parish was declared vacant and Fr Joseph Joy Dean, a cousin of Henry Joy McCracken, was appointed as parish priest.

Shortly afterwards Fr Myles' creditors reappeared, and he had to leave the Isle of Man to seek voluntary exile in France, where he died in 1840.

The foundation stone of the church of the Blessed Virgin Mary in Chapelizod was laid in 1843. The building at Chapelizod was a chapel-of-ease for Blanchardstown. Things were financially very difficult for parishioners during these lean years. In spite of poverty, disease and famine, however, they rallied. When we look at these magnificent buildings we should reflect on the years in which they were built and respect the efforts of our forefathers.

It is not surprising that during the famine years there appears to have been considerable hardship in the barony. There are records of thefts of food, disease and an increase in the number of deaths. There was a cholera epidemic in the county. The barony of Castleknock, however, did not suffer as greatly as Finglas, where many deaths occurred. A previous visitation of this disease in Blanchardstown in 1830 claimed many lives.

Fr Dungan appears to have been involved with the Repeal movement under Daniel O'Connell – and got his knuckles rapped for it by Archbishop Murray. Around this time the Young Irelanders attempted to rally support for their cause in Blanchardstown, but due to poor organisation only sixteen people turned up to their meeting.

WAKING THE DEAD

There was an attempt at this time to discourage the custom of waking the dead. These *wakes* were often an excuse for drunkenness and licentiousness; at times they were dangerous, particularly if the corpse had suffered from cholera, typhus or some other infectious disease.

The Irish Folklore Commission list the following games that were played as wakes in the Blanchardstown area: - The Grass that Grew Crooked around the Crooked Crab-Tree, Band Master, Bird Lost, Chew, Chew the Button, My Man Jack, All Hampers on the Block and Little Bit of Fish. Most of the games were harmless and designed to keep those at the wake house from falling asleep. On occasions there was excessive drinking at wakes and some of the games had slight sexual connotations and there was a certain relaxation in the interaction between the sexes. In fact it was often said that a wake was often followed by a wedding.

One custom often carried out at wakes was that earth from the grave was put in the coffin and prayers said. A variation of this was where earth was blessed and brought to the burial and thrown on the coffin. It referred back to the time when the Penal Laws prohibited a Catholic priest officiating at a funeral in an established church (i.e. Church of Ireland) churchyard. Few Catholic churchyards were in existence at that time because of the Penal Laws. When the coffin was brought out it was put on four chairs before being lifted by the bearers. The chairs were then knocked over and the cortege moved off. The bearers had a hierarchical system of relay in carrying the coffin, depending on the closer the degree of relationship or friendship with the deceased. Many of the bearers carried salt in their pocket as a charm.

The houses along the funeral route drew blinds and in latter years when people had radios they were turned off all day. Another tradition was that if a person was coming from the opposite direction they would join in the cortege for at least three steps.

At the churchyard if two funerals were approaching the gates it was a matter of honour to get in first. So the sedate respectable funeral often degenerated into an unseemly scramble. Another point of honour was that the gravediggers, then usually friends and family, would have the grave filled in and the earth tamped down before the prayers finished.

Nowadays unfortunately it's not unknown for a motorist to cut in on a funeral cortege or to pass out a hearse – an unthinkable act then.

There is an old Dublin expression for a 'toucher' or 'sponger': 'He's a friend of the corpse'. The expression goes back to the time of these customs, when drink was freely available at wakes. A professional mourner would appear with tears in his eyes and professions of intense grief. The greater the display of grief the more generous the measure of whiskey poured by the bereaved for the 'toucher'. 'Who is he? Someone might ask, and the response invariably was 'Sure he must be a friend of the corpse'. Although he might be a stranger to friends and family he was never challenged lest offence be given to the deceased, who probably never knew him. The efforts of the clergy to suppress wakes did not achieve their purpose, as they still continue today, albeit with a little more decorum.

THE PARISH REGISTER

The Parish Register for Blanchardstown goes back to the 1750s. Some of the names listed in it are still prevalent in the locality today: O'Brien, Farrelly, Mulligan, Roe, Bolger, Duffy, Mullally, Tuite, Sweetman, Reynolds, Magrane, Butler, Askins, McGuire, White, Mullin, Payne, Bell, Magenis, Byrne, Corrigan, Smyth, Murray, McKenna, Boyle, Dempsey, McMahon, Carberry, Powderly, Murphy, Kelly, Sherlock, Phelan, Carmichael, Muldoon, Farrell, Connor, Mahon, Horgan, Shiels, Martine, Hackett, Mulloy, Gaffney, Linard, Dillon, Connigam, Bermingham, Magan, McCormick, Richardson, Brady, Corcoran, Beaker, Campbell, Christie, Lison, Leary, Doyle, Leneghan, Caffrey, Monaghan, Bronon, Clarke, Carroll, Naughton, Reilly, Collins, Connell, Dixon, Fitzpatrick, Halfpenny, Carpenter, Staunton, Casey, Segrave. All of these names were recorded before 1774.

EMPLOYMENT

Most of the local men would have worked as farm labourers and in related work such as horse-wrangling, cattle-droving, herding, gardening and so on. There was also employment in Rathbornes and various mills in Blanchardstown, the Lower Road and Ashtown. Some work would have been available in road-making, and the canal and railway also provided employment. There were plenty of pubs and sheebens (up to thirteen) in the locality in the early 1800s, serving a population of 854. Sole traders such as smiths, cobblers, builders, millers and shopkeepers helped boost the local economy. Tradesmen had lots of work and there would have been a fair degree of self-sufficiency. The army, navy and constabulary were other sources of employment. In fact the British army was really the Irish army, with many of the rank and file, together with a fair proportion of the officer class, being Irish. It is not generally known that the Irish language was widely employed in issuing orders at Waterloo. Wellington and most of his troops were Irish. Although it must be said that Wellington disowned the land of his birth with a memorable phrase 'if you were born in a stable, it would not make you a horse.'

THE BAND

The St Brigid's Brass Band, founded in 1826, is the oldest village band in Ireland. In 1922 the Band's brass drum was discovered in the Tolka following an explosion when the local courthouse was blown up; the band's practice rooms were part of the courthouse. The anti-Treaty forces had nothing against music; it was the judiciary of the new Free State that they had no time for. The band provided music at O`Connell's huge rally at Tara in 1843 and again at the fiftieth-anniversary commemoration of Easter Week in Dublin in 1966. On this occasion they led a contingent of 1916 veterans past the saluting base at the GPO.

I was in the parade with the Pearse battalion who provided the FCA guard of honour. As the serried ranks of the 1916 veterans, led by the Blanchardstown Brass Band, approached the saluting platform, arms swinging, shoulder high, heads erect, marching in time to the stirring martial airs they gave the eyes right to President de Valera who was taking the salute. It was hard to believe that most were in their 70s.

The Blanchardstown Brass Band (St Brigid's Brass Band)

PORTER'S GUIDE AND DIRECTORY FOR BLANCHARDSTOWN 1912

Porter's Guide and Directory for North County Dublin describes Blanchardstown as a very pleasant village in the barony of Castleknock, about five miles from the General Post Office, Dublin. Population about 150. The principal industries are the Flour Mills of Mrs Delany, the manufacture of rugs, stair carpets, mats and altar surroundings at Lester's Mills, and the making (wholesale) of bakers' and confectioners' fats at the Margarine Works. The village is remarkably clean and well arranged. There is an excellent National School, also a Post Office, a Constabulary Station and Public Telephone Call Office. Petty Sessions are held every alternate Monday. The Railway Station is about a quarter of a mile from the village. The Catholic church is a very neat edifice, with three altars, gallery and very fine organ. The church is capable of accommodating about 600 worshippers. The Very Rev. Stephen Fennell, PP, and Rev. John Healy, CC, are the officiating clergy.

Magistrates Attending Petty Sessions – William Bobbett, Patrick Donegan, R.W. Rathborne, John Hone Willan, Gavin Low, Edmund Mooney, Joseph Mooney, H. St George. Held on 9 January and fortnightly after. Clerk, G.A. Malley, Chapelizod.

RIC Constabulary – Michael Harrison and 4 constables.

St Brigid's National School – New school, built in 1891. Average attendance about 120. Mrs Mary Jane McDonnell, Principal; Miss Mary McDonnell, 1st Assistant; Mrs Margt. McDonnell, 2nd Assistant.

Post Office – Money Order, Telegrams, Savings Bank, Annuities, Parcel Express, Miss Donohoe, Postmistress.

BLANCHARDSTOWN RESIDENTS

(B) Boylan, Raymond J., Draftsman. Bradley, J., Station Master. Brien, William, Shoeing and General Smith and Repairer of Agricultural Implements. British Margarine Co., Ltd., Manufacturers of Bakers' and Confectiones' Fats (wholesale), and at 10 St Helen's Place, London, E.C. Thos. E. Checkfield,

Manager. (C) Carr, William, Farmer.Checkfield, Thomas E., Castleknock. Corcoran, Thomas, Spirit Merchant and Farmer. Cullen, John, Horse Dealer. Cunard, Alexander, Corduff House. (D) Delany, Joseph, Ltd., Millers and Corn Merchants, and at 119 to 122 Thomas Street, Dublin. Donnelly, Miss Mary M., Vintner and Farmer. Donohoe, Patrick, Sand Contractor and Provision Dealer. Donohoe, Miss Margt., Grocer and Provision Dealer. Doyle, Bernard, Grocer. (E) Ellis, Miss Mary, Shopkeeper. (F) Fennell, Very Rev. Stephen, P.P., The Presbytery. (G) Grogan, Mrs Corduff. (H) Healy, Rev. John, C.C., Blanchardstown. Hoey, Henry. (L) Lester, C.S., Manufacturer of Rugs, Mats, Stair Carpets and Altar Surrounds, Avon Carpet Works, Telegrams: Lester, Blanchardstown. (M) Maguire, Michael, Farmer, Coolmine. McDonnell, Michael, National Teacher, Moy Mell. Moore, Thomas, J.P., Ashtown. Murphy, Wm., Farmer, Corduff. (O) O'Neill, Mrs Mary, Wine and Spirit Merchant, Blanchardstown House. (Q) Quin, John, Carpenter, Corduff Cottage. (R) Rahill, Michael, Wine and Spirit Merchant, Farmer, Coal and Provision Merchant, Phoenix Park House. (T) Thornton, Robt., Spring Lawn.

RATHBORNES

No local history of the barony could ignore the impact the Rathbornes had, not only in Castleknock, Blanchardstown, and Ashtown but in Dublin as a whole. The first Rathbornes arrived in Dublin in the early 1400s and settled in Christchurch, moving to Stoneybatter in 1636 and setting up in Dunsinea in 1744. They are unquestionably the oldest candle-manufacturing company in Europe and possibly in the world founded in 1455. The process by which they made candles involved dipping cotton wicks hung on circular frames called dippers into a molten mixture of wax. The wicks were dipped up to a hundred times until the required thickness was reached. The earliest surviving candle was found near Avignon and dates from the first century AD. Candles were known as far back as 5000 years BC, however. Time-keeping candles, which burnt the hours marked on the candle, were used from the ninth century and continued to be used in coal mines up to the mid-1940s to measure the duration of shifts.

In the late 1700s a substance, known as spermaceti, found in the head of sperm whales was discovered to be a better material for candles than beeswax. In 1823 stearine was found to produce a better light but in 1857 paraffin wax, a by-product of crude petroleum, was revealed to be suitable for the manufacture of candles in moulding machines.

Eamonn MacThomáis, in an article written about the Rathborne family, mentions a Richard Rathborne, who quit the business and became a clergyman 'and thus spent his life lighting them instead of making them'. The factory in Dunsinea known as Phoenix Candleworks was destroyed by a fire in 1895. In was, however, rebuilt and operations continued there until 1925, when the firm moved to East Wall. The Rathborne family lived at Dunsinea and at Scribblestown House at different times and were connected through marriage with the famous mathematician Sir William Rowan Hamilton, director of the neighbouring Dunsink Observatory. Many local people were employed by Phoenix Candleworks and indeed there were stepping stones on the Tolka that were for years used as a short cut to work. The property is now occupied by An Fóras Talúntais.

THE MILL ASHTOWN

This old mill on the side of the canal is visible for miles around, and has been there since the early decades of the nineteenth century. The mill was originally driven by water taken from the canal along the mill-race. It was used at the turn of the century for processing by-products of flax such as linseed oil and cow-cakes. The Ronuk Company later used it for manufacturing floor polish. Later on it manufactured hair oil, which came in long narrow bottles with a cork.

Until recent times the side of the mill carried an inscription advertising Rodeo polish – a brand name for the firm's product. The clock which was on the wall of the mill is said to have come from Newgate prison. The mill yard

The Mill, Ashtown
Photograph by Brendan Campion

was supposed to be haunted by the sound of ghostly horses – the galloping hooves and the jingle of the harnesses echoed eerily as the horses made their nocturnal journey to somewhere unknown, for reasons on which mortals need not dwell. Up the road, the St Eloi Works – or to be more prosaic, the Ashtown tinbox factory – operated from 1930 until recently, and gave much employment in the area. St Eloi was the patron saint of tinsmiths.

BLANCHARDSTOWN MILLS

There were two mills in Blanchardstown – one on the canal, the other on the Tolka. The mill on the canal was originally a woollen mill constructed around the same time as the canal, using canal waterpower. It converted to steam power in 1878 and began to mill flour, employing a beam engine. This was an early form of stationary engine and was much commented on at the time.

The mill was taken over by the British Margarine Factory in the early 1900s. They delivered their produce in a Foden steam wagon, which attracted huge attention as it was the first seen on Dublin streets. The Crest company took over in 1972 and moved to Ashtown following a disastrous fire in 1994. Blanchardstown Mills was on Mill Road near the hospital and also had retail outlets around Dublin. The Blanchardstown Mill drew its power from the Tolka River. I recall mills shops on the North Circular Road, Phibsboro, and also on Main Street, Blanchardstown, laid out in the style of bygone years, with flours and spices of every description displayed. Their headquarters then was in Thomas Street and the firm was owned by the Delaney family. The whole area was ideal for milling, with the Liffey, the Tolka and the Canal providing the waterpower. There was even a small windmill in Diswellstown that was used for pumping water. In addition, an ancient mill in Castleknock called the Red Mill or the Baron's Mill was worked by John Sprotton in about 1650.

COWBOYS – ROYAL AND OTHERWISE

Sir John Blacquire built Deerfield, the handsome house now used as the US ambassador's residence, with state funds in about 1775–76 for £8,000 and sold it back to the state six years later for £7,000. Sir John was chief secretary and also held the post of bailiff of Phoenix Park, which allowed him to graze his substantial herd of cattle on these lands free of charge. He was nicknamed 'the king's cowboy'. Whether his building or bovine 'stroke' brought about his nickname we can guess at – surely the latter. But there were many real cowboys in the area.

The cattle market on the North Circular Road near Prussia Street (previously at Smithfield) gave regular employment to drovers from all around Castleknock, Blanchardstown, Finglas and Cabra. Much of the land around the area was used for lairage, (overnight facilities) for cattle and sheep on their way to market.

Wednesday was market day, and a constant stream of sheep and cattle headed south down all the roads from early morning. I can still remember the music of bleating sheep and lowing cattle acting as a gentle alarm clock. The cattle people, who earned their living droving, buying and selling, were the salt of the earth. They worked hard, often drank hard and sometimes fought hard. The cold, damp and exhaustion of long journeys, mostly in the dark of night, never affected their humour. The cattle families, like the Costellos, Kavanaghs, Lyons, Connells, Brannigans and Ennises to name but a few bring back memories of a bygone era.

6

ABBOTSTOWN, DUNSINK, CABRA AND ASHTOWN

ABBOTSTOWN

The Abbot family were Norman settlers, who having given their name to the area, have left nothing else to record their deeds or contributions to the barony. Thomas Serjeant, who married Joan Tyrell, one of the sisters of the last baron of Castleknock, appeared to live in Abbotstown in about 1400. Serjeant's surname was probably derived from his family's occupation as deputy sergeants to Henry Tyrell of Castleknock, who was chief sergeant of the county of Dublin in the early decades of the thirteenth century. 'Chief sergeant' was a feudal title just below that of 'knight'.

The proprietors of Abbotstown during the Down Survey of 1655 were 'Sir John Dungan, Irish Papist, and Ignatius Mapus Protestant', each holding about sixty-six acres. In the survey of the part of Abbotstown owned by Dungan, mention is made of one thatched house, several cottages and the walls of an old chapel. This chapel appears to refer to Caeveen churchyard. Following the Restoration, a family called Long appears to have been in possession of it. The Longs were officers in the Irish army of that time. Mention of a Richard Hanlon is also made in a will relating to the estate. The estate then fell into the possession of a Kilkenny family called Sweetman at the end of the seventeenth century. The Troy family, of which Archbishop Troy was the most illustrious member, had Kilkenny connections, and Dr Troy was on good terms with a John Sweetman, who subsequently designed the pro-cathedral.

The next owners were the Clements' family, ancestors of the earls of Leitrim and famous for the fact that one of their number was Nathaniel Clements, chief ranger in Phoenix Park. It is his residence, Áras an Uachtaráin, that is today home of our president. Then Sir William Rowley, an admiral, was a tenant on the estate. The banking family Falkiner, represented by Frederick Falkiner, next settled here. The family hailed originally from Leeds but were well domiciled in Ireland at this stage. Frederick's father, Daniel, was MP for Baltinglass and even served a term as lord mayor of Dublin. Frederick's wife was a Hamilton of the famous Hamilton family from Coronary, County Cavan, who were ancestors of Lord Holmpatrick.

The family originated in Scotland and gave service of a military and political nature to successive administrations. Frederick's eldest son, Daniel, a barrister, inherited the estate in 1782. Daniel's son Frederick John Falkiner, became a baronet when only twenty-two and became MP for Athy having been nominated by his relative the duke of Leinster. Frederick Falkiner was resolutely opposed to the Act of Union and refused all bribes of money or title to induce him to support it. Falkiner encountered financial problems of raising and equipping an infantry regiment of which he was honorary colonel and died in Naples in 1824 in tragic circumstances. He left no children.

It should be noted that many Anglo-Irish gentry and the Orange Order opposed the Union, whereas many Roman Catholic ecclesiastics and clergy, including Dr Troy, supported it. The former thought they would lose power and privilege; the latter thought the act would bring about an amelioration of the Penal Laws, if not indeed full Catholic emancipation.

HOLMPATRICKS

The Hamilton family at adjoining Sheephill bought the Falkiner property in 1832. They had come to reside in the area in the late 1790s and built their fine house at Sheephill, afterwards known as Abbotstown, on the amalgamation of these properties. This house numbered amongst the great residences of County Dublin and was a little to the north of the Falkiner's house of Abbotstown, which was demolished. The Hamiltons appear to have been a prolific crew – one of their number, James, married three times and fathered thirty-six children. This was long before John Logie Baird's invention provided an alternative though less productive use of one's time.

Hans Hamilton was MP for Dublin in 1797 and, like his cousins the Falkiners, was in total opposition to the Union. Hans was a captain in the Fifth Dragoon Guards. He was an MP for twenty-five years and always headed the poll. He married twice and had one son, James Hans Hamilton, who was twelve years old when he succeeded to the estate. James was elected MP in 1841 and held the seat for twenty-two-years; he was universally liked.

During a debate in the House of Commons, Daniel O'Connell, in one of his characteristic put-downs, referred to James Hamilton as 'Muttonhead from Sheephill'. Ion Trant Hamilton, James' second son, a Cambridge graduate, inherited the estate because Hans James, the eldest brother, died young. Ion represented the county from 1863 until 1885; his views in favour of the union were as strong as his grandfather's were against it. On Queen Victoria's jubilee Ion was ennobled as Lord Holmpatrick, a title derived from lands the family held near Skerries, County Dublin. He married Victoria, the granddaughter of another famous Dubliner, Arthur Wellesley, duke of Wellington – or 'nosey', as he was better known by his soldiers. Holmpatrick's son, Hans Wellesley Hamilton, who had an uncanny similarity in features to his great-grandfather the Iron Duke, pursued a military career and avoided politics. He fought in the First World War and was awarded the MC and the DOM. He helped

Abbotstown House
Courtesy of Fingal County Council

Frederick Falkiner of
Abbostown
Courtesy of Fingal County
Council

James Hamilton of Sheephill
later known as Abbotstown.
He married three times and
fathered thirty-six children.

Courtesy of Fingal County
Council

found the Irish Hospitals Sweepstake, became involved in Sir Patrick Dunns Hospital and was a patron of the Scouting movement and of King's Hospital. He became a member of the LDF (forerunner of the FCA) during the Second World War and loyally served in the reserve force of the Irish army until his death in 1942.

There is a very old yew tree on the lands of Abbotstown which local people call the 'begging tree'. Hans Wellesley Hamilton Lord Holmpatrick, had an arrangement whereby he would be at the yew tree on a certain day each week to meet with local people, to discuss their problems. He would then give them advice and more often than not, a little money to help them out – hence the name the 'begging tree'.

His son, then only in his teens, found the upkeep of this large estate too difficult. The introduction of death duties had a devastating effect on big land-owners. The duties charged on the valuation of the estate meant that many of the landed class, who were 'land rich' and 'money poor' had to sell their land to release the money to pay the death duties. As it would be well known why the land was being sold, it would be open to 'predatory purchase' so the land would not get a fair market price. He sold the portion of the estate that is now used by the Department of Agriculture, having lost the remainder to the Department of Health, who set up the James Connolly Memorial Hospital on the demesne after their compulsory purchase of it in 1947. The hospital was originally a sanatorium for the eradication of tuberculosis.

On 16 November 1949 Mr Fitzgerald, in a Dáil debate on the provision of sanatoria (note correct Latin plural), asked the Minister for Health Dr Noel Brown 'If he will state (a) the present position concerning the proposed erection of a regional sanatorium in Blanchardstown, County Dublin, (b) the size of the proposed institution, (c) the approximate cost and (d) when site development works are likely to commence.'

Minister for Health Dr Brown, then a member of Clann na Poblachta, replied:

> I have accepted the tender of Messrs. Hussey, Egan and Pickmere (Ireland) Ltd., for site development works at Dublin Regional Sanatorium, Blanchardstown, County Dublin. The proposed institution has been planned to contain 508 beds and to accommodate 8 doctors and 150 nurses and the requisite staff in 30 separate buildings on a site of about 240 acres. The approximate cost of the sanatorium is expected to be in the region of £1,400,000. Site development works were commenced by the contractors this week.

In Dáil Éireann on 18 February 1954 Noel Browne, now a Fianna Fáil deputy, asked the Minister for Health to name the new chest hospital (note – no longer sanatorium) after James Connolly. The Minister for Health said it would be a matter for Dublin Corporation as they would be taking over the hospital but he would bring it to their notice. Dr Ryan, the minister, actually tended Connolly for his wounds in the GPO in 1916.

The opening was performed by T.F. O'Higgins Minister for Health. Both James Connolly's son Roddy and daughter Nora were present at the opening ceremonies for the hospital on 22 April 1955. The site comprised over 240 acres of woodland and park from the Abbotstown estate and would previously have formed part of the Great Scaldwood of Blanchardstown. The hospital was largely reconstructed in recent years and is now known simply as Connolly Hospital, Blanchardstown.

St Francis Hospice Raheny are presently fundraising for a new hospice to be built on a site within the hospital grounds at Abbotstown. It is expected that building will commence shortly.

In 1803 Hans Hamilton laid the foundation stone for the rebuilding of St Brigid's church in Castleknock, and there are memorials to the Hamiltons,

Dunsink Observatory
Photograph by Brendan Campion

later Lord Holmpatrick, in the church, and the family tomb in the churchyard. The spire, erected in 1864, was dedicated to Hans Hamilton. It unfortunately had to be removed in 1957 as it had become unstable.

Thomas Ellis of Abbotstown had a girls school in Abbotstown demesne in the 1820s, and similar arguments over the religious instruction of Catholic children occurred there, as in Porterstown. Hillbrook, near Abbotstown, was the home of Robert Sampson, who died in 1764. He was a lieutenant colonel in the army and had connections with Donegal. One of his ancestors represented that county in parliament. Elm Green was owned by Richard Malone, an art collector; in 1837 its owner was F. Dwyer. In modern times the Barrett family occupied Elm Green until Fingal county council acquired the house and lands for development of a fine eighteen-hole public golf course that is there today.

CAEVEEN

This disused graveyard, with its ruined church, has a forlorn and mysterious air about it, all the more so now that the road leading to it has disappeared in motorway improvements. It was at a sharp corner on what was once the road from

River Road to Dunsink. At the point where one crosses the bridge over the Tolka (Bockey's Bridge), the stump of an old tower hung precariously on the edge of a cliff. This was a tower for watchmen who guarded the graveyard against resurrectionists, a class of ghoulish criminal, who sold mortal remains to the medical colleges for research and experimentation in less enlightened days. Further up the road was a well; in 1727, Rutty the antiquarian called it St Commergan's Well when he reported that it was used by locals for curative qualities. The well was just outside the graveyard, and Lord Holmpatrick had it covered in. This was not a complete success, as the roadside always had a small trickle of water running down its side.

The name of the ancient church and graveyard was thought at one time to refer to St Kevin (Caoimhín), but there is no tradition to connect him with the locality. There is a theory that in *The Book of Leinster* a poem refers to relic Aeda Finn (meaning 'grave of fair Hugh'). This became corrupted to 'Caeveen' the 'c' in relic was retained, leaving Caedh finn, or 'Caeveen'. The poem went on to refer to nine score priests and 5,000 noble persons awaiting resurrection there. This fair Hugh was also known as 'Mo-aedh-oc' and was a great friend to St Onchu – who may have brought relics of the priests and nobles referred to.

In 774 and again in 836 there is mention in *The Annals of the Four Masters* of Viking raids on Cluain Mór Maedoc which could refer to Caeveen. The last burial there, according to oral tradition, was in about 1925; the person interred was called Keogh. The most recent gravestone, however, is dated 1866. The association of the name 'Aedh' or 'Hugh' with such place names as Mulhuddart and Caeveen, together with the story of Aedh Mac Morna's battle against Cumhal at Cnucha, may indeed indicate pre-Christian origin to the name. Walter, the brother of Archbishop Troy, is buried here; this gave rise to an incorrect local belief that Archbishop Troy was buried there.

DUNSINK

A short distance from Caeveen is Dunsink, whose name is taken from that of an ancient dún (or 'fort'). The small hillock in a field a few hundred yards from Caeveen may be the dún in question. There was also the remains of what appeared to be a huge ring fort in the field opposite the observatory, however. The field, which later became Dunsink tiphead, was known for generations as the Rath field and could have been the location of the dún. Across the fields from there was a fine castle, belonging to the Woodlocks and later the Dillon family, on the road to Cappagh, but no trace of this castle remains. The observatory was built in 1785 with legacy money from Francis Andrews, provost of Trinity College. Rev. Henry Ussher, the learned astronomer, selected Dunsink for both its vantage point and its distance from the Dublin air, which even then was smog-laden. Dunsink does not have as much precipitation or cloud as its surroundings; part of Howth Head enjoys a similar microclimate.

Ussher also designed the instruments and planned the buildings and their layout. He died in 1790; his successor, John Brinkley, later bishop of Cloyne, carried out important mathematical research. He was an expert on ecclesiastical law and one of the great astronomers.

William Rowan Hamilton, a Dubliner, succeeded Brinkley at the age of twenty-one. He discovered the theory of quaternions while on a ramble along the Royal Canal banks at Broombridge and carved the following into the stonework: i (squared) = j (squared) = k (squared) = ijk = −1.

This conclusion flashed through his mind: geometrical operations in three-dimensional space need quadruplets not triplets. This was the most significant mathematical discovery of the age. Hamilton was a child prodigy. At the age of five he could translate Latin, Greek and Hebrew. He spoke Syriac at twelve and Persian at fourteen. He died in 1865, at the age of sixty.

Francis Brunnow, who replaced Hamilton, erected a new telescope and was responsible for the installation of many new technological instruments. His special work was the study of the parallax of stars. Robert Stowell Ball was a tutor to Lord Rosse's children in Birr, where the largest telescope in the world was at that time. Ball moved to Dunsink as Brunnow's successor. He brought in a new telescope for photographing stars and other sophisticated equipment. He was a keen horticulturist and introduced many new and rare species of plants to Dunsink gardens.

Arthur Alcock Rambaut and Charles Jasper Joly (famous for his photographs of the corona during the eclipse of the sun in 1906), Edmund Taylor Whittaker (one of the most brilliant mathematicians in the world), Henry Crozier Plummer, Charles Martin, H.A. Bruck, M.A. Ellison and P.A. Wyman followed these earlier pioneers and made significant contributions to the fields of astronomy, science and mathematics. Famous guests who visited Dunsink include William Wordsworth and Sir Walter Scott. It has been bypassed since then by more modern observatories, where viewing conditions are optimal. But we should not lose sight of the immense contribution Dunsink has made to the study of our universe.

Dunsink has been marred by the ugly tiphead and scrapyards, and what was once a lovely country lane has degenerated into an eyesore. Dunsink Lane – or Long Lane, as it was known – was reputed to be haunted by a large mastiff with glaring red eyes as big as saucers. A road connecting Dunsink with Barn Lodge was called the New Road despite being laid during the Famine as relief work. The motorway now intersects it. In nearby Scribblestown lived Lady Eva Forbes, sister, of Lord Granard. Her gleaming black Ford limousine was much commented on in an era in which pony and trap were the norm. As I write, Fingal County Council are beginning to clear this area for recreational use.

CAPPAGH HOSPITAL

Nearby Cappagh Hospital was founded by the Religious Sisters of Charity in 1908 and is renowned for its orthopaedic surgery. The lands on which it is built were known as Heathfield and were formerly the property of Sir Richard Martin. His widow, Lady Martin, willed the property to the Sisters on her death in 1907. Lady Martin was the daughter of Sir Dominic Corrigan, the noted cardiac physician, who lent his name to the medical terms 'Corrigan's Pulse and Corrigan's Button'.

In the grounds of Cappagh Hospital is the high altar that was placed on O'Connell Bridge for the 1932 Eucharistic Congress ceremonies.

Cardiff Bridge about 1936
Courtesy of Fingal County Council

CARDIFF'S BRIDGE

On the road to Cabra now skirting the boundary of the barony of Castleknock we cross Cardiff's Bridge, named for the Kerdiff family, whose ancestors arrived with the Normans. There was a spade factory and mill here, and many of the workers came down from the Newry area to work in it. There was a pub here – a coaching inn called The Jolly Topers. Wrestling matches took place on a Saturday afternoon outside the premises and legendary bets were made. The pub ceased trading in the early 1920s.

During the 1930s there was a burst of geological activity on the riverbed; a foreign visitor was intrigued with the dashing on a Blanchardstown wall and suspected its source may have been associated with precious stones. Whether or not the Diamond rush at Cardiffsbridge (the source) realised its prospects has been a mystery ever since. Perhaps the true wealth of the Tolka was the fantastic fishing to be enjoyed there – it was teeming with the finest brown trout.

Cardiffsbridge was a little village until the mid-1950s. I recall as a child looking at the devastation wreaked on the cottages that used to adjoin the bridge here by a horrific flood in December 1954. Unfortunately, in the headlong pursuit for profit, real values such as clean, living rivers were allowed to die. The Tolka, however, is fighting back – and winning.

Little Cabragh House (locally called Lord Norbury's), demolished in 1939. It was home for a while to Lord Norbury, the notorious 'hanging judge', and belonged to the Segrave family for generations
Photograph Fingal County Council

CABRA

The Dominican Convent in Cabra was built on Segrave land in 1819. The nuns were originally in Channel Row and after a short time in Clontarf they moved to Cabra and founded a school for boys and girls there. Fr Thomas McNamara, the famous Vincentian, discussed with the Dominican Order the idea of a school for deaf girls around the same time as the Christian Brothers were in discussion with him for a school for deaf boys. The result of these discussions is today's St Gabriel's School for deaf girls and St Joseph's School for deaf boys. This convent today manages national schools, secondary schools, schools for the deaf and a facility for the blind and deaf. There is a story told that about a hundred years ago thieves broke into the convent chapel and stole the sacred vessels, including the Sacred Host. The thieves got hopelessly lost in the grounds and, fearing their sacrilege was preventing their escape, emptied the chalice on the ground and still unable to escape, threw the chalice at a tree. A small oratory has been built where the host fell in the grounds, and a plaque with the outline of a chalice inscribed on it was fixed to a tree.

At the time of the Down Survey, a Mr Agart owned the land at Great Cabragh (the present Convent lands), which comprised 130 acres, while Henry Segrave held Little Cabragh, which comprised 60 acres. Part of these lands was previously owned by the Kerdiff family, who sold it to the Plunketts and later to Christ Church Cathedral, which in turn leased it to John Parker and later to Francis Agart. The Kerdiffs held on to their land in Pelletstown and Dunsink in the reign of Elizabeth I.

Following the Restoration, Benedict Arthur came into possession of Great Cabragh, and he was followed by his son John, who was a relative of the renowned Dr Thomas Arthur. John inherited not only the estate library but his father's clock watch as well. In 1687 a clock watch, or indeed any luxury, would have meant more than land. Land was seen as almost an undisposable asset for family reasons, tradition and so on, and plate, pistols, horses (blood stock), jewellery and clothes were more highly valued than it. Land was something peasants worked, under the supervision of an overseer, and from which an income was derived. The aristocracy only saw the cake and spurned the bread, which was the basis of life.

John Arthur, a Catholic, died in 1733, lucky to still be in possession of his land. His son, Benedict, however, had converted to the Established Church ten years previously and married a close relation at the age of seventeen. This marriage resulted in correspondence between Archbishop King, Church of Ireland archbishop of Dublin, and the English hierarchy in a debate fuelled by John Arthur, the father of Benedict. Benedict died in 1752, after which his children let the house to Thomas Waite, under-secretary at Dublin Castle. The estate was then purchased by the Segraves, who already owned Little Cabragh.

CABRAGH HOUSE

The Segraves' main house was on the present-day intersection of Fassaugh Avenue and Ratoath Road. They lived there for centuries, their name 'See Graf' ('sea lord') indicating a German or Scandinavian origin. The house was built in about 1597 and was 'surrounded by several gardens, orchards and parks planted

Cabragh House, now Dominican Covent, Cabra
Courtesy of Fingal County Council

with ornamental trees'. It was built of stone and had tiled roofs. There was a brewery, dairy, stables, barns, malthouse, coach house and byre, where the family arms were displayed in wood carvings. There were twelve bedstead chests bound with iron, carpets, tapestry, canopies of taffeta and silk, oil paintings and so on. The house was later designed to hide priests on the run and had secret passages, a false chimney and a priest's chamber.

The loyalty of the Segraves to the crown was not in doubt – witness their ability to hold on to their possessions. One member of the family, a Capt. James Segrave, fought Hugh O'Neill in single combat during the Battle of Clontibret. O'Neill was overpowered by Segrave's superior strength, but just before Segrave delivered a coup de grace, O'Neill mortally wounded him with his dagger and the Irishman won the day. John Segrave, a colonel in the Irish Volunteers, died and the property passed to Denis Daly (Lord Dunstable's father) for a short while.

The next occupant, Lord Norbury (John Toler), had an evil reputation; his name is reviled to this day as that of the 'Hanging Judge'. At one session he sentenced 198 prisoners to death by hanging. He began his bloody career as an MP for Tralee; he became MP for Gorey in 1790 and later Phillipstown (Daingean). During his political career he was prominent in his opposition to Grattan's Catholic Relief Bill. He had been admitted to the bar in 1770, and as a strong supporter of the government, was given due recognition for his services, he attained many offices, including that of lord chief justice, and was eventually ennobled as earl of Norbury.

Lord Norbury was born in County Tipperary in 1745, his father having been a Cromwellian settler there. The senior Toler, Daniel, was married to Letetia Otway of Templederry, a member of a well-known Anglo-Irish family. The Tolers originated in Norfolk. Daniel Toler, as High Sheriff of Tipperary, involved himself in a conspiracy to judicially murder a priest, Nicholas Sheehy. He had him arraigned on a charge of administering secret oaths in connection with the Whiteboys. After being acquitted and walking free, Sheehy was arrested on a new, trumped-up charge of aiding and abetting a murder. This time Toler packed the jury and Sheehy and another man were executed. It appears that not only was Sheehy innocent of the crime but that in fact the crime never occurred. The 'murder victim' was alive and well and residing in Limerick city.

John Toler, the son, later Lord Norbury, had poor legal skills though he had a formidable knowledge of literature and used his

Lord Norbury (John Toler), the 'hanging judge' Courtesy of National Portrait Gallery, London

knowledge to intimidate lawyers and defendants who were unfortunate enough to come before him. He had a very sarcastic wit and a twisted sense of humour, and his courts were like a wild theatre. In one case a youth appearing before him observed Norbury reaching for his black cap. (The black cap was donned by judges before imposing a death sentence). The youth pleaded with Norbury to give him the 'long day', a colloquial name for a life sentence. 'I am happy to oblige you', retorted Norbury, 'I will give you a stay of execution until tomorrow – the longest day of the year'. The fact that the trial was held on 20 June afforded Norbury an opportunity to parade his perverse humour. On another occasion, while passing a death sentence on a young pickpocket convicted of stealing a watch, he dryly remarked 'you grasped for time now you've caught eternity.'

An instance of Norbury's contempt for law was illustrated in a trial where a Capt. Frazer slashed an elderly cottier to death with his sabre. The unfortunate victim was repairing a cart outside his own front door when the drunken officer came across him and murdered him for allegedly breaking the curfew. The coroner's jury found a verdict of wilful murder. Toler, overturning the verdict, sarcastically remarked that if the victim were as decent a man as he was represented to be it was well for him to leave this wicked world behind but if he were as wicked as many others in the locality, it was as well the world was shut of him.

Another story tells of John Philpott Curran, the famous lawyer, who was addressing the court when the furious braying of an ass penetrated the walls of the building. Norbury banged his gavel and intoned 'One at a time, Mr Curran'. Curran got his own back at a bar dinner when Norbury asked if Curran thought the meat was tough.

Curran retorted, 'You try it, my Lord, and indeed it will be well hung'.

Norbury's acerbic wit was also directed as his own peers. Dining with a member of the gentry who was much given to exaggerating his hunting prowess, his companion informed the table that he had shot thirty-one hares before breakfast! 'My God, Sir!' exclaimed Norbury, 'you shot a wig!'

At dinner a lady seated next to him initiated some small talk with Norbury about the inclement weather and he dryly replied 'Sure winter has come to pass the summer with us.' Another time having tasted a rather fine port, a favourite tipple of his, he remarked, 'This is port for calm, any port in a storm'.

Norbury was a short man had a jovial demeanour, with tiny grey twinkling eyes and a peculiar mannerism of puffing out his cheeks in a blowing motion to punctuate his sentences. This habit attracted the nickname the 'Puffendor' for him. He had a strong, deep voice that was at odds with his diminutive stature. He was an accomplished duellist and even challenged the lord lieutenant at eighty years of age when under investigation for having slept on the Bench during a murder trial. Napper Tandy, the noted United Irishman, challenged him to a duel, which failed to proceed. His most famous trial was that of Robert Emmet, in which Norbury continually interrupted and abused Emmet. Daniel O'Connell heartily despised him and described him as a judicial butcher and a buffoon. O'Connell initiated the investigation of his conduct in the trial where he fell asleep.

A Blanchardstown woman whose husband Nobury had unjustly sentenced to hang cursed him on her deathbed, and he suffered from insomnia from that time onwards – though not in court. He died in his bed at the age of eighty-five in 1831. At his burial it was discovered that the ropes lowering his coffin were too short. While runners were sent for replacements an onlooker shouted 'get plenty of rope boys, he never spared it on others.' There were reports of his ghostly appearance in Cabra, galloping on horseback down the Ratoath Road in the dead of night. Other stories say his ghost takes the shape of a huge mastiff that has glaring, bloodshot eyes and drags clanking chains.

Norbury owned an estate at Durrow near Tullamore, County Offaly which his son Hector Toler, second earl of Norbury inherited. He was shot dead in 1839 near his home. No one was ever apprehended. The Toler line included Hector John, the third earl who had a daughter Elizabeth Graham Toler whose son was Field Marshal Sir Harold Alexander Earl Tunis, a very famous general in the Second World War.

The Segraves again took possession of Cabra House after Norbury's death. Charles Segrave was the last of the family to reside there, vacating the property in 1912. His son Henry was a famous racing driver, winning both the French and Spanish Grand Prix. For a time he held the land speed record, achieving 231 mph in 1929, and he is credited with inventing the crash helmet. He then took up motor-boat racing and won the European Championship, achieving the world record in his boat *Miss England I*. He was killed while bettering his world speed water record on Lake Windermere Friday 13 June 1930. He was recorded just before the accident at 101.11m.p.h. The house was demolished in 1939 and the site was left idle for years, until flats for senior citizens were built there. These flats were named after Canon Valentine Bourke, PP of Cabra West, who was an accomplished violinist, who did tremendous work in the area and was an extremely charitable man.

There was, however, a little part of the Segrave residence still in use until recently: a good, panelled door hanging in the house where this writer was reared. During the demolition, a workman relative with a good eye for value liberated it from the desired official destination. During recent renovations it unintentionally ended up in the original destination from which it was saved in 1939 – the city dump. Lord Norbury's fine Chippendale table has a grander home, however: it is used in the state apartments in Dublin Castle for state banquets.

BLACKHORSE LANE

Blackhorse Avenue formerly Blackhorse Lane (or simply 'The Lane') was the main Navan coach road. The Navan Road is relatively new and at one time a section of it was known as Windy Arbour. At the junction of Blackhorse Lane with Nephin Road there was a picturesque thatched cottage with an orchard full of mouth-watering, juicy fruit. The house was unfortunately destroyed by fire in recent years and rebuilt without the thatch. At the adjacent Cabra gate of the Phoenix Park there was a well, known as the Poor Man's Well.

The first hostelry we encounter on the road to Castleknock is the Hole in the Wall, famous as the longest pub in Europe. This public house got its name from the time when the British army was 'under canvas' in the park before embarkation for France in the First World War. The thirsty troops would slip down, unnoticed, for a pint through the turnstile or the hole in the wall. A previous owner of the pub was Jim Clancy, who was a famous draughts player. The owner before him was Nancy Hand, and the pub traded under her name before it was the Hole in the Wall. The Blanchardstown band used to march here on St Patrick's Day in years gone by, when beating the

The Hole in the Wall, Blackhorse Lane
Painting by Phil Parker

parish bounds was a custom. They would play some Irish airs and return to Blanchardstown. The records are very coy as to whether refreshment was offered – St Patrick's Day was legally dry at the time. All pubs were closed and the only place alcohol was served was at the dog show. The present owner, P.J McCaffery, has gathered a fine collection of Guinness memorabilia and antiques dating back to when Daniel O'Connell graced the mahogany of the hole in the wall while quenching his thirst. Blackhorse Lane was a very close-knit community with a real village atmosphere; it was said that the villagers were so close that they spoke their own language.

The next inn, the Turnstile (a new name referring to the turnstile gate opposite), was originally the Elm Grove Inn and was previously owned by Jim Comiskey, and before that by the Baggot family, one of whom was a Nationalist MP. This family had a contemporary portrait of St Oliver Plunkett at their home here.

On the left-hand side of Blackhorse Avenue, heading towards town, near Ashtown Gate, was a curious construction: a stone platform with three steps leading up to it. At first glance it looked like a milk-churn stand. Closer inspection, however, revealed a little design or crenellation on the wall. The story goes that it was built for Archduchess Elizabeth von Hapsburg, the empress of Austria-Hungary. Elizabeth, who was regarded as the most beautiful princess in Europe, married Franz Joseph, the emperor at the age of seventeen. She was the daughter of the Bavarian duke Maximillian Joseph of the Wittelsbach line and suffered from a neurotic restlessness – a strain present in this family. She spent a great deal of time travelling abroad and visited Ireland in 1879 and 1880, staying in Summerhill, County Meath, the seat of Lord Langford. She was an accomplished horsewoman and rode a black hunter called Domino.

When Elizabeth – or Sissi, as she was universally known – went riding in Phoenix Park, these steps were provided so she could mount and dismount at ease. Elizabeth's son Rudolf died in the suicide pact at Mayerling with his lover Baroness Maria Vetsera. Elizabeth herself was assassinated in Switzerland in 1898. An item worth relating is that on each of her visits, the government of Austria-Hungary wrote in advance to the registrar-general at Dublin Castle for a report on the state of public health in Dublin. In an example of bureaucracy gone crazy, Dublin Castle continued to send this report to Vienna and Budapest long after her death and only ceased to do so at the start of the First World War.

Elizabeth, Empress of Austria used this platform to mount her horse before \riding in the Phoenix Park, 1879-80
Photograph by Fr Eugene Kennedy

ASHTOWN

In the thirteenth century, Ashtown was owned by the priory of St John the Baptist outside Newgate. Richard Netterville then came into possession of the land when the monasteries were dissolved by Henry VIII. The Down Survey of 1655 notes that 'John Connell, Protestant, owned 200 acres. There is upon the premises one castle with two thatch houses valued by the jury at eight pounds. There is also a small orchard'. These Connells appear to have been ancestors to Daniel O'Connell, the Liberator. The castle referred to is Ashtown Castle, which later became the under-secretary's house and, more recently, the nuncia-

King Edward VII [on the right] visits the Phoenix Park races
Courtesy of Fingal County Council

ture. The nunciature building had become prey to dry rot and had to be largely dismantled. During this work the original castle, which had been hidden by extension and alteration, was discovered. It has since been refurbished and is now open to the public.

In 1663 John Connell sold 152 acres for inclusion in the deer park that the earl of Ormonde was creating, and that would later be known as Phoenix Park. The remainder of the lands were inherited by Maurice Connell, but they became crown property in 1688, possibly in return for land in Iveragh, County Kerry, and were given to Thomas Keightley J. Dunne, Esq., of Ashtown is mentioned as being a major landowner here in the mid-1800s. The Levins-Moore family owned Ashtown House, and Ashbrook was owned by Lieutenant Col Dugdale in the early 1900s.

It was rumoured that it was at Dugdale's house that the British army general staff in Ireland met after the 1916 Rising and that it was there the decision was made to execute the leaders of the rebellion as an example to others. The men executed did become an example – but not of the kind the general staff wanted. The execution appalled the people and instilled an awareness of nationalism that brought about the withdrawal of the British from most of the country following the War of Independence. The family name of Lord Ashtown was that of Trench, from Sopwell Hall County Tipperary, Woodlawn County Galway and Dunboyne, County Meath. Fredrick Trench, MP for Portarlington, became the first Lord Ashtown in 1800.

The Walton family, of music fame lived on the River Road in Ashtown Lodge for many years. A more recent celebrity to live in the area was the film producer Kevin McClory. The Phoenix Park racecourse was opened in 1902; the founder members were Sir John Arnott, J.H. Peard and Major Eustace Loder. In 1903 Edward VII and Queen Alexandra attended a meeting at the Phoenix Park to wild acclaim. There was a special clock installed – an Australian invention, that allowed communication by electrical means between the starting gate and the judges box. The first race was held back until 3 pm to allow the royal couple attend a review of troops in the Fifteen Acres.

That royal visit produced another local yarn. One of the riders was supposedly asked to pull his horse and allow the king's mount to win. The story goes that the rider refused to do this and in doing so suggested that this royal person and all his kin were born without benefit of matrimony, among other things, and that he should (to paraphrase politely) make love and travel, preferably back to England. Following this outburst he went on to win the race. He was then blacklisted and never again allowed to race. His mind became unhinged and for years afterwards he could be seen cycling along the Navan Road, beating his bicycle with a riding crop. This is a good story but I can find nothing whatsoever to authenticate it.

The Phoenix Park racecourse was originally used for both steeplechasing and flat racing. There is an underground reservoir in the grounds, and this water was drawn off in pipes along the course to alleviate problems caused by summer droughts. The big race of the year was the 1,500 Guineas; the racecourse unfortunately no longer exists, however. The Phoenix Park racecourse is now a residential complex of apartments mainly.

The Navan Road, Ashtown, was the site of two very well-known schools: the Morgan school for boys and the Mercer school for girls. The latter was founded by Mary Mercer on the site of Mercer's Hospital, but she decided the building was not a suitable site for a school and in 1734 granted it for use as a hospital. Although she died the following year, a school was opened in Rathcoole in 1747 according to instructions contained in her will. A Richard Morgan died in 1784 and left a will which contained instructions to set up a boys and a girls school for poor Protestants. The boys school opened in 1813 and the girls moved over from Rathcoole thirteen years later. These institutions later became fee-paying schools for Protestant children. The two schools were eventually absorbed by Kings Hospital, and their original location is now a halting site. The sports grounds were acquired by St Brigid's GAA Club and are a great asset to the community. St Brigid's GAA Club celebrated their seventy-fifth anniversary in 2007.

'ON A COLD DECEMBER DAY'

As the ballad recalls, 'A duel commenced on Ashtown Road' on 19 December 1919. A section of the Dublin Brigade of the Irish Republican Army under the command of Paddy Daly lay in wait at Ashtown Cross. Their target was Lord John Denton Pinkstone French, Field Marshal and viceroy since 1918. French, a prototypal blimp, in appearance red-faced and white moustached, had risen to the rank of field marshal and had been commander of the British Expeditionary Force in France at the outbreak of the Great War. He was eventually relieved of his post to the relief of all except the enemy in December 1915. The ambush party included Sean Tracey, Martin Savage, Mick McDonnell, Tom Kehoe, Seamus Robinson, Dan Breen, Sean Hogan, Joe Leonard, Tom Kilcoyne and Paddy Daly. Breen, Tracey, Robinson and Hogan were on secondment from the Tipperary Brigade.

The ambush was laid on direct orders from Michael Collins. The volunteers cycled out to Ashtown in twos and at intervals so as not to arouse suspicion. Some weeks previously a permit order was introduced by the authorities stipulating that each motorcar must display a photograph and the name of the driver to prevent the transport of arms and ammunition by the IRA. The unit regrouped at Kelly's Public House, Ashtown, close to the railway station where French was due to arrive at 12.45p.m. before travelling in convoy by car to the

*Volunteer Martin Savage who died
in the Ashtown ambush
Courtesy of Fingal County Council*

Viceregal Lodge in Phoenix Park. This top-secret information was passed on to Collins' intelligence department by a highly placed agent in Dublin Castle.

The plan was to push a heavy farm cart across the narrow Pelletstown Road near its junction with the Navan Road thus slowing down the convoy en route to the park. The attack would be mainly directed against the second car in the convoy, which was usually occupied by Lord French according to IRA intelligence.

The unit, having taken up position, spotted a Dublin Metropolitian policeman place himself at the centre of the crossroads in order to control traffic. At the same time four military lorries passed down the road to the station. Savage, Kehoe and Breen approached the farm cart and lifted the cart off the shafts and started to push it across the road. The cart was heavier than expected and the trio had difficulty pushing it. The policeman shouted at them to halt their progress explaining his excellency was due to pass. Breen shouted back at him threatening him. Whilst this altercation was going on one of the party, positioned behind the hedge, lobbed a Mills bomb at the policeman. It exploded, throwing Breen and the policeman on the ground, wounding the police officer in the foot.

Meanwhile the motorcyclist leading the convoy flashed past followed by the first car. Shots were exchanged between the ambush party and the occupants as the car accelerated past. However, the IRA volunteers concentrated all their firepower on the second car believing it to contain Lord French. Bullets whistled around the crossroads and the explosion of the Mills bombs rent the air, which became diffused with the blue acrid smoke from the grenades. Breen was wounded in the leg by rifle fire and, almost immediately, Martin Savage, who was standing beside him, suddenly collapsed in his arms having been wounded in the lower face and neck, and died almost instantly. Shortly afterwards the military broke off firing and this allowed Breen and the others to escape.

The wounded policeman, a young Leitrim man, Con O'Loughlin, lay on the ground while some local people attended to him. Martin Savage, twenty-one years of age from Ballisodare, County Sligo, a veteran of the Easter Rising, also died. Detective Sergeant Halley, who was in Lord French's car, was shot in the hand and was taken to King George V hospital (now St Bricin's) for treatment. Dan Breen was treated for his leg wound by Dr J.M. Ryan, captain of the Dublin Hurling Team.

Because of the restrictions for using of motor vehicles the IRA had only short arms and Mill bombs available on the day. One could hardly cycle up the Navan Road with a rifle strapped to the crossbar of a bike. The lack of firepower against the formidable arms available to the military lessened the chance of success. Lord French was not in the second car as the volunteers were led to believe; he was in the first car that sped so quickly away. The police constable's intervention, causing one man to panic and throw the grenade, gave advance warning to French's convoy.

The attack was universally condemned. County councils passed resolutions. Bishops fulminated and the newspapers of the day railed against these 'miscreants', 'ruffians', 'scoundrels', 'gunmen'. There was little or no public support from the Dáil or Sinn Féin deputies. The Sunday evening after the ambush thirty men under the command of Peadar Clancy entered the premises of the *Irish Independent*, one of the most vitriolic in their condemnation, and destroyed printing presses with sledgehammers.

The post mortem on Martin Savage took place in Bessborough Barracks (just inside the Ashtown gate of Phoenix Park), which ironically had been closed down the week before the ambush. The coroner suggested to the jury they find that the killing of Martin Savage was a case of justifiable homicide in self-defence. The jury declined his advice returning a verdict that the deceased was killed by a military escort and voted an expression of sympathy to the deceased family. It also revealed that Sergeant Rumble of the 2nd Berkshire Regiment fired the fatal shot that felled Martin Savage.

Local lore had it that the evening of the ambush the Black and Tans descended on Ashtown and lined all the males over eighteen years of age against the walls of the handball alley with a view to shooting them as a reprisal but the Black and Tans did not arrive in Ireland until March of the following year.

Some weeks later Breen met Maud Gonne MacBride and Charlotte Despard, two of the most doctrinaire republicans of their day. Madam Despard upbraided Breen for taking part in the ambush against her brother Johnny, Lord French.

Dan Breen went to New York for a while some years later and describes in his book *My Fight for Irish Freedom*, how he bumped into Con O'Loughlin the DMP man who helped foil the ambush. O'Loughlin was out of work and broke. Breen, through his republican contacts, got him fixed up with a job as night watchman.

There was a small outhouse to the left of the Halfway House but on the righthand side of the road leading to the station a plaque was affixed marking the spot where Savage died. The memorial has since been moved three times because of road-widening schemes.

Ballad of the Ashtown Ambush

(sung to the air of The Snowy-Breasted Pearl)
'Twas a cold December day
A lorry ploughed its way
'Midst bullets splash and play
On Ashtown Road.

In that car a living tool
Of England's hated rule
There was begun a duel
On Ashtown Road.

Young Savage, unafraid
With gun and hand grenade
Attacked them undismayed
On Ashtown Road.

But a bullet laid him low
From a rifle of the foe,
That's another debt we owe
For Ashtown Road.

But another day shall dawn
Like that cold December morn
When a martyr's name was born
On Ashtown Road.

We laid him in a grave
Where the willows sadly wave
Oh! Son of Erin brave
Farewell to thee.

The famous handball alley was at the rear of the Halfway House. According to local folklore the cement used on the court wall was supposedly mixed with the blood of cattle to give it strength. The finest exponents of handball in the country played there, including Tom Delaney and his brother Dinny, Matt and Larry Daly and Denis Lacey. Other famous characters in the history of handball associated with the alley were: – Jim Clarke (father of John, Austin, Jim and Frank Clarke), T. Aldridge, Pat Lyons (one of the all-time greats), Tim Hurley and M.J. Kelly. There was also a big following in Ashtown for the local soccer side, Elm Rovers, who even had a song written in their honour that was sung at football matches. They had a playing field which later became a pitch-and-putt course and which is now Martin Savage Park.

The Halfway House was built in the mid-1800s by a man called John Fox and was later owned by a Mr Doyle, followed by Peter Kelly and then by his son Giles Kelly. Myo O'Donnell, who was related to the Kellys, worked here before buying McKenna's public house in Castleknock, supposedly for £13,850 in the early 1960s. The Halfway House is now owned by Con Tracey and is one of the most famous landmarks in the area. A fine collection of old prints of the area decorates the walls.

7

PHOENIX PARK
'GO UP TO THE PARK ... '

James Butler, twelfth earl and first duke of Ormonde (1610–1688), was appointed lord lieutenant in Ireland in 1662. Earlier, as a lieutenant general, he had defeated the Catholic confederate armies at Kilrush and New Ross in the 1641 Rebellion. In the Civil War between parliament and the king, he supported Charles I. He fled to France after the defeat of the royalist cause and the subsequent execution of Charles. Butler returned to England with Charles II on the restoration of the monarchy. During his period in office as lord lieutenant of Ireland he made vigorous attempts to encourage Irish industry and commerce. It was his idea to acquire and enclose the land we know today as Phoenix Park, as a deer park and a recreation area for all the king's subjects.

The king's mistress, Barbara Villiers, duchess of Cleveland, had persuaded Charles II to grant her the Phoenix Lands, but Ormonde somehow got him to revoke his decision. When the duchess discovered what had happened she harangued Ormond, saying that she hoped she would live to see him hanged. He sweetly replied that he would like to live long enough to see her ladyship grow old. He died in 1688 aged seventy-seven, she in 1709 aged sixty-eight. It was envisaged that the Park would comprise the lands of the former Kilmainham priory, which included Inchicore and Islandbridge, as well lands on the north side of the Liffey that included Newtown, Phoenix House and part of Chapelizod. This area was eventually extended to include Castleknock and Ashtown.

In an earlier chapter there is reference made to Connell of Ashtown (Pelletstown), whose land was acquired for the park. Christopher Fagan parted with the Phoenix lands and Alderman Daniel Hutchinson with the Newtown lands (roughly the area known as the Fifteen Acres, together with the zoo and Áras an Uachtaráin). The earl of Ormonde engaged a builder named William Dodson to build a wall surrounding the park in 1663–64. The wall, however, like its biblical counterpart in Jericho, came tumbling down. (The slang term 'jerry-built', meaning poorly constructed, may derive from the story of Jericho, but other derivations have been suggested). Dodson was advanced huge sums to repair the walls in spite of his poor workmanship and use of bad stone. Dodson eventually offered to keep the wall in repair for £100 per annum. It was discovered some years later that he had sub-contracted the work for £30 per year. The park was stocked with fallow deer brought in from England, along with partridge and hawks. The red squirrel, along with the grey squirrel, are also foreign introductions. The red squirrel became extinct in Ireland, and English animals were imported. The grey squirrel was an American import.

The building of the Royal Hospital Kilmainham, on Phoenix Park land south of the Liffey, reduced the size of the park. The fact that the public Lucan road, running through the park alongside the Liffey, gave ease of access to poachers (mostly soldiers stationed in Dublin augmenting their meagre

Wellington Monument, Phoenix Park, circa 1890

rations), resulted in a decision being made to build a wall along this road on the north side of the Liffey. Sir John Temple of Palmerstown, the solicitor general, was given the task and received £200 and the land between the Liffey and the road for his pains.

The park has not changed much in area since: it now covers about 1,752 acres. The walls are seven miles long, and nine major gateways have access to vehicular traffic at Castleknock, Ashtown, Cabra, North Circular Road, Parkgate Street, Islandbridge, Chapelizod, Knockmaroon and White's Gate. This last gate is seldom open nowadays for environmental reasons and traffic restrictions. There are also turnstiles at several locations.

Credit must be given to the earl of Chesterfield for most of the developments that imbued the park with the magnificence it retains to this day. Chesterfield became lord lieutenant in 1745. His brief was to smother the Irish with kindness. Our Gaelic cousins in Scotland were causing problems for the Hanoverian dynasty that ruled in England by their support for the Stuart succession to the throne. It was therefore good politics to keep the Irish on side and mollify them to some extent, lest they revive their Jacobite sympathies. This policy was not entirely successful, as many Irish flocked to the standard of Bonnie Prince Charlie. Chesterfield laid out tree lined walks and fine straight roadways and opened the park to the people.

The magnificent tree-lined avenue leading from Parkgate to Castleknock, a distance of 2.6 miles, is named for this popular viceroy. He also erected the fluted Corinthian column Dubliners call the Eagle Monument and what is officially known as The Phoenix Column. The names and origin of both arise from a mistake. The name of the Eagle Monument arises from the fact that the phoenix has a similar appearance to that of an eagle. Most Dubliners in 1747, when the monument was built had never heard of a phoenix. They had probably never seen an eagle either, but the idea of an eagle was easier for them to grasp, so the edifice became in popular parlance 'the Eagle Monument'.

The Phoenix Column came from the impression the authorities had, or wanted to create, that the park was named after Phoenix House, the manor which was the nucleus of the park, thus ascribing the origin of the name

City Arms, Dublin.

The Phoenix Column and Viceregal Lodge in the Edwardian era
From a postcard from Chas. L. Reis & Company

Phoenix to the original owner of the manor, Sir Edmund Fisher. The explanation for this was that the site and prospect of this manor house, which had been built where there was nothing before, was symbolic of a phoenix rising from the ashes. This origin of the name was often held locally to be true.

In the Down Survey, Ashtown's bounds are 'on the east with Little Cabragh, South with Ffenix on the west, Castleknock on the north the Toulchy (Tolka) water'. The Ffenix refers to the *fionn uisce*, or 'fair water', which was eventually corrupted into 'Phoenix', from which the name of the park is derived. Most reports suggest that the *fionn uisce* was a well and variously locate it as being near the magazine fort (previously Phoenix House) or being in the zoo grounds. Another source gives the location as inside the gate of Áras an Uachtaráin, and yet another mentions the Poor Man's Well at Cabra Gate.

I feel that, as it is described as a boundary, this 'well' must be the stream which has its source at Deerpark and continues underground, paralleling the main road, slightly to the left, in the city direction. It surfaces as the pond at Mountjoy corner, again as the pond in Áras an Uachtaráin, as the small lake in the zoo and as the pond in the People's Gardens before entering the Liffey near the railway tunnel. The Fionn Uisce was joined by a tributary that had its source in what is now Ratoath Estate. It passed the rear of Convent View, continued along the boundary of Pope John Paul Park, went under the road at the aptly named Brook shop, passed the front of Roosevelt Cottages and met the main stream at Áras an Uachtaráin. The Poor Man's well was probably connected with this.

There was a chalybeate spa between the pond in Áras an Uachtaráin and the zoo lake that was patronised by the duke and duchess of Richmond. Trees were planted around it, it was surrounded by brickwork and a dome was placed over it. There was seating around the spa for those taking the waters. The charge for the water was a penny a glass. There was a stone tablet erected inscribed as follows: 'This seat was given by her Grace, Charlotte, Duchess of Richmond, August 19th 1813'.

The spa fell into disuse about 1880, possibly because its flow was diminished as a result of drainage work and contamination. The site of the spa has been identified as being behind the sea lions' pool in the zoo. At one time there was a serious proposal to change the name of the park to Kingsborough Park.

PORTER'S GUIDE AND DIRECTORY FOR PHOENIX PARK 1912

The Phoenix Park, situated immediately on the boundary of the City of Dublin, is the largest park in the United Kingdom, having an area of about 1,700 acres and is over seven miles in circumference. At one time it was the property of the Knight Hospitallers, but on the suppression of the monasteries it was surrendered to Henry VIII, and afterwards constituted a deer park by the duke of Ormonde in the reign of Charles II. The earl of Chesterfield, when lord lieutenant of Ireland, made several additions and alterations and opened it as a place of recreation and amusement for the inhabitants of the city. There is a magnificent granite obelisk to the memory of the duke of Wellington and an equestrian statue to Lord Gough. It contains the residence of the lord lieutenant (viceregal lodge), the chief secretary and the under secretary of Ireland, the Hibernian School for Soldiers Children, the Ordnance Survey, the Zoological Gardens, Royal Military Infirmary and the Royal Irish Constabulary depot.

Phoenix Park National School – Mrs J. Reidy, Principal; Miss G. Gillman, Assistant. Average 60; on rolls, 78

National Schools, Chapelizod (Protestant) – Mr Bradley. Average 30; on rolls, 40.

PHOENIX PARK RESIDENTS

(A) Anderson, Robt., Bailiff, Whitefields. (C) Connell, J., Concrete Lodge. (D) Dougherty, Right Hon. Sir James, Under Secretary's Lodge. (G) Godden, Fredk., Head Deerkeeper. Gordon, Samuel T., Surgeon to the RIC Depot. Green, Max, Private Secretary's Lodge. (M) McInnes, P., Board of Works, The Cottage. (N) National Schools, Mrs Reidy, Head Teacher. New Lodge, Vice-Regal Lodge. (P) People's Gardens, Robert Seaman, Curator. Power, Samuel, Belleville House. (R) Royal Hibernian Military School, Col Deane, Commandant. Royal Irish Constabulary, Mr O'Connell, Commandant. Royal Magazine Fort., Lieut. Playfair, Superintendent. Royal Military Infirmary, Col C. Birt in charge. (S) Salter, J., Weir View, Island Bridge. Sherlock, Patrick, Springfield House. Smith, James, Dairyman. (V) Vice-Regal Lodge – His Excellency the Earl of Aberdeen. Chief Secretary – The Right Hon. A. Birrell, M.P., (U) Under-Secretary – The Right Hon. Sir James B. O'Dougherty. (Z) Zoological Gardens, Capt. Arbuthnot, Superintendent.

'... AND VIEW THE ZOOLOGICAL GARDENS'

The Zoological Society of Ireland, was founded in 1830, and at first was granted five acres of land in Phoenix Park by the lord lieutenant, the duke of Northumberland. The zoo, which now covers 13 hectares, is recognised as one of the most picturesque – it is also amongst the oldest – in the world. Decimus Burton, was the architect responsible for the layout of the gardens, is credited with the design of the old gate house, with its thatched roof. He also designed several of the gate lodges in the park. The first animal tenant of the zoo was a

Rama, a mail elephant, with his keeper Mr McNally and his trainer Capt. Harrington
McNally was killed by another elephant named Tita in 1903

wild boar, and he was joined later by a sambar deer, emus and ostriches. Early gifts to the zoo (or the 'azoo' in Dublinese) were a lioness, a leopard, a moufflon (a wild horned sheep), a hyena and a wolf, the benefactor being King William IV. The zoo is not only noted for the number of animal species it contains but for the layout of the gardens, and the plant species would do credit to any botanical garden. Over the years Dublin Zoo became famous for breeding. Approximately 600 lion cubs were born there. The lion filmed in the trademark of MGM Films was apparently a jackeen also, coming originally from Dublin Zoo.

A strange fact is that, with so many wild animals in captivity, there were only two human fatalities. The first involved a reindeer that gored its keeper, and the other involved an elephant called Tita that stamped on his keeper. Tradition has it that an umbrella stand was made from the beast's foot. The beautiful cedar (*Cedrus Atlantica*) inside the main gate and a copper beech (*Fagus Sylivatica Purpurea*) beside the reptile house were planted by Queen Victoria on her royal visit in 1900.

The Old Gate Lodge, Dublin Zoo designed by Decimus Burton
Photograph by Brendan Campion

The zoo is as much a botanical garden as a zoo, with specimen trees and shrubs from all over the world. The African Plains project, creating a savannah for large animals, is a highlight of a visit to the zoo.

THE HOLLOW

Across from the main entrance to the zoo is a natural amphitheatre with a bandstand in the middle known as the Hollow. This was a regular Sunday-afternoon venue for Dubliners. It reached the zenith of its popularity during the early 1890s –1900s with brass bands from the different British regiments playing martial airs. The St James Brass and Reed Band was one of the foremost civilian bands. This band's selection of Irish airs and music-hall favourites attracted huge audiences, which availed of the special tram laid on by the Dublin United Tramway Co., who sponsored the bands.

The Father Mathew Band, York Street Band, Junior Army & Navy Stores Band, Boys Brigade Band and Wellington Quay Band were among the other

The Duke of Marlborough unveils the Gough Memorial
From the Graphic, *13 March 1880*

The Band Stand and Hollow, Phoenix Park. A popular Sunday afternoon musical outing for
Dubliners as much now as in yesteryear
Photograph by Brendan Campion

more notable bands to grace the Hollow. While the crowd listened to the music, hawkers plied their trade, selling toffee-apples, 'Peggy's leg', fizz-bombs and other delicacies. The adjacent tearooms were also a great attraction – as they still are today, providing refreshments in the most picturesque Victorian surroundings.

AROUND THE PARK

At the Ashtown gate there are two lodges, the one on the right being formerly Bessborough Police Barracks. A short distance away is the Phoenix Park Special School. This was formerly a national school, and many children from the area attended it. The school was built in 1848 and is a very quaint building. At the rear of Áras an Uachtaráin is Ratra House, the headquarters of the Civil Defence Corps. This was originally known as The Little Lodge or The Concrete Lodge and was the residence of the private secretary to the Viceroy. At one time it was occupied by our first President, Dr Douglas Hyde, on his retirement from office. Ratra was the name of Dr Hyde's former home in County Roscommon.

WINSTON CHURCHILL'S CHILDHOOD IN PHOENIX PARK

In the year 1876 Lord Randolph Churchill, his wife the former Jenny Jerome and their son Winston came to live in the Little Lodge at the rear of Áras an Uachtaráin. The arrival of the Churchills coincided with the appointment of the sixth Duke of Marlborough as lord lieutenant of Ireland. Lord Randolph was the son of the Duke of Marlborough and was brought there to act as his father's private secretary. The 'promotion' of the Duke of Marlborough had its origin in a marital scandal involving Edward Prince of Wales. Randolph had information concerning the prince, which he threatened to use if a divorce case in which his brother Blanford was named as co-respondent, was not dropped. In reaction to this attempt at blackmail Prime Minister Disraeli, on Queen Victoria's authority, offered Marlborough the lord lieutenancy on the basis that he and his family would do a greater service to the crown by increasing their distance from court. The job offer could not be declined and, to add to her majesty's and the exchequer's satisfaction, the position involved unreclaimable expenses of £40,000 per annum for a salary of £20,000 per annum.

Lord Randolph would not have been unfamiliar with his brother's difficulties, as he did not have strong views on marital fidelity either. In his case it resulted in a greater penalty than temporary exile, as he eventually died at the young age of forty-six from general paralysis. His wife, Jenny Jerome, daughter of New York financier Leonard W. Jerome, was a woman of rare and exotic beauty. She was reputed to be of Iroquois descent and her looks were said to derive from this source. This Native American bloodline was often mentioned by Winston Churchill particularly on his travels in the UK and Canada. While living in Dublin, Jenny gave birth to another son, John Strange Churchill. Speculation was rife at the time concerning his parentage as Jenny was alleged to have had more than a passing acquaintance with one John Strange Jocelyn and she had a reputation of having similar views as Randolph's vis-à-vis the openness of marriage.

Winston grew up as a fairly lonely child, absorbed for hours on end deploying little tin soldiers in various military formations. He had little contact with either parent, not an unknown occurrence in well off circles at that time. Indeed, I recall my father introducing me as a child to an elderly man from Blackhorse Lane, and telling me that this man used to play marbles with Winston Churchill. Meaning nothing to me at the time I cannot remember the man's name now. Perhaps some reader can help identify him.

Churchill mentioned later on in life that his first memory was of his grandfather the Duke of Marlborough, unveiling the statue of Lord Gough in Phoenix Park. Churchill outlived the statue which was blown up in 1957 by 'an illegal organisation' as the newspapers of the day quaintly put it.

The deprivation of parental affection that Winston Churchill experienced was more than compensated for by the devotion of his nanny, Mrs Everest. In his memoirs, he relates an incident that occurred while astride his little donkey. Accompanying his nanny through the Park, she espied a military formation

The Gough Memorial, circa 1890.
Note the policemen with Bobby helmets and the soldier in the carriage with Pillbox hat
Photograph from the Lawrence collection, courtesy of the National Library of Ireland

marching towards them. As they drew closer she noted the dark green uniforms and immediately thought – Fenians? She took to her heels, Winston and donkey in tow. In the ensuing pandemonium Winston was thrown from his mount, landed on his head and suffered slight concussion. As it turned out the uniforms were the bottle green ones of the RIC on parade from the nearby depot. Churchill cited this event as his first introduction to Irish politics and a painful one at that.

A more sombre recollection of his was receiving the present of a drum from a Mr Burke. Some years later, when back in England, he learned of the assassination of the same Mr Burke and Lord Cavendish in Phoenix Park. He also had a memory of a great fire that destroyed the old Theatre Royal in Hawkins Street in 1880. As a young man he went on to report on the Boer War as a military journalist where he was captured and subsequently escaped. He later on got into a few 'scraps' against the Boers in the company of the Dublin Fusiliers. He became involved in politics, eventually embracing the concept of Home Rule in Ireland. He accepted the inevitability of the exclusion of four Ulster counties on a temporary basis.

However, the First World War intervened and, in Ireland, the 1916 Rising, the conscription crisis, and the rise of Sinn Féin raised the ante and it was Independence not Home Rule that was on the agenda. War commenced and Ireland was plunged into suffering and bloodshed. British Rule in Ireland became untenable. Churchill proposed a solution based on his premise 'Get three Generals if you cannot get three Judges,' and launched the Black and Tans and Auxiliaries on Ireland. During this time he would brook no criticism of these forces and defended their actions in spite of overwhelming evidence of atrocities. Yet, when the chance came for a truce in 1921, he more than any other of the cabinet spoke forcefully in favour of it. King George V had made his opinion known that he was personally shocked and embarrassed at the behaviour of the crown forces in Ireland and this may have affected Churchill's stance.

During the subsequent Treaty negotiations Churchill was very tough, gave very little and pushed very hard, supporting Lloyd George's threat 'of immediate and terrible war'. Although aloof at first during the negotiations, he engaged Michael Collins in some banter. Collins at one stage remonstrated with Churchill as to how the British had hunted him down night and day and even put a price on his head. Churchill responded by showing Collins a similar proclamation the Boers had issued about himself in 1899. Collins broke out laughing and thus an awkward moment passed.

Churchill continued to play a role in Irish affairs giving support to both Griffith and Collins and the Provisional Government while also aiding Sir James Craig's government in Belfast. Churchill was hopeful that the Boundary Commission might succeed in an agreed United Ireland, albeit with Dominion Status within the Commonwealth, and with limited powers. Many students of history and politics have debated as to whether or not Churchill was a friend to Ireland. The issue probably never crossed the mind of Churchill himself. His sole concern was Britain and her empire, and every other nation's welfare was only incidental. He saw the freedom of Ireland as a gift bestowed by imperial benevolence and not a right to nationhood by entitlement, and indeed the nature of the gift was a loan. He said as much in his infamous speech at the close of the Second World War when he praised 'the restraint and poise' exercised by the British government in relation to neutral Ireland. '(We) never laid a violent hand upon them even though at times it would have been quite easy and natural.' Eamon De Valera replied, 'Mr Churchill makes it clear that in certain circumstances he would have violated our neutrality and that he would justify his action by Britain's necessity – if accepted, it would mean that Britain's necessity would become a moral code and when this necessity became sufficiently great other people's rights, were not to count ...'

Eamon De Valera had hit the nail on the head. It was a moral code, and not only Churchill's but that of the whole ruling class in Britain and was the essence of empire.

Churchill died in 1965. Ten heads of state and representatives of one hundred and twelve countries, including former IRA chief-of-staff Frank Aiken who was then minister of external affairs for the Republic of Ireland, attended his funeral.

I have not addressed Churchill's status as world statesman and war leader in the Second World War, not through neglect or omission, as I only wanted to treat his relationship with the country for which was a while his 'home' country. Incidentally, his ghost in the form of a child has reportedly been seen in Áras an Uachtaráin the former viceregal lodge when his grandfather the duke of Marlborough held court.

The next building on the right was formerly Cabra garda station, and before that it was the viceregal laundry. So, the first occupants cleaned up grime and the next occupants cleaned up crime! Continuing on, the visitor will find on the right the zoo and on the left the back entrance to McKee (formerly Marlborough Barracks). Contrary to popular lore, the plans for the building did not get mixed up with those for a barracks in India.

The building was designed by Lieutenant Col J.T. Marsh as a cavalry barracks with an eye to the training opportunities in the nearby park. The famed Army Equitation School is attached to the barracks. The original mast for transmitting Radio Éireann was also sited there. The next building, garda HQ, was formerly a training depot for the gardaí before they moved to Templemore; before that it fulfilled a similar purpose for the RIC. It was built between 1839 and 1842. The depot included a riding school for policemen – an illustration of how history can repeat itself.

The People's Gardens close by were laid out in 1864 and are renowned for the colourful spectacle provided by the many species of flowering plants displayed there. The rose beds in particular host a glorious display in summer. Charles Gavan Duffy, Thomas Davis and John Blake-Dillon decided to found the *Nation* newspaper after a meeting there. The adjoining Parkgate Street area was the site of the county gallows.

The Wellington monument or more properly the Wellington Testimonial across the main road from the Peoples' Gardens, towers over the park from a height of 205 feet. It was designed by Robert Smirke, RA, and was once the tallest obelisk in the world. The obelisk in Washington DC, although 555 feet high, was not built until the 1880s, whereas work on the Wellington monument commenced in 1817 – but was not finished until 1861. The plan originally was to locate it in St Stephen's Green, and there was much debate before it was finally decided to place it in its present position, on what was formerly a saluting battery. Cannons were placed here on ceremonial occasions and roared a welcome on royal visits and similar events. Dubliners, with their typical wit, dubbed the Wellington Monument 'the overgrown milestone' but for generations of Dublin children it was known as the 'Slippery Steps' owing to the difficulty in scaling the eleven steeply sloping steps. The railway tunnel on the line between Heuston Station and Connolly runs under the park very close to the Wellington monument.

On the left-hand side of the main road facing Castleknock is the Citadel Pond, known universally by the more accurate and less pompous name of 'The Dog Pond'; a section of the canine population of Dublin performs their ablutions there. This was also a great skating pond in winter when we had them. It rarely ices over now. During the Second World War a German aircraft dropped a bomb here in error. Back at the crossroads an intentionally dropped domestic bomb removed the equestrian statue of Lord Gough on July 22 1957. The explosion was so violent it was heard over a large area of the city.

THE 'INVINCIBLES'

On a Saturday evening 66 May 1882 Under-Secretary Thomas Burke and the newly appointed chief secretary, Lord Frederick Cavendish, were assassinated on the main road, Chesterfield Road. They had earlier attended the inauguration ceremonies in Dublin Castle connected with the succession of John Poyntz Spencer, fifth earl Spencer, KG, to the lord lieutenancy of Ireland. (He was responsible for introducing barbed wire to Britain but Diana, Princess of Wales, was to bring greater fame to the Spencer family).

Lord Frederick Charles Cavendish, newly appointed chief secretary to Ireland, and Thomas H. Burke, under secretary were in attendance. On the conclusion of the formalities they set off separately for the viceregal lodge (now Áras an Uachtaráin). Cavendish left on foot shortly after 7 p.m., followed some while later by Burke travelling by cab. Burke caught up with Cavendish at Park Gate Street and alighted from his cab. They continued on their way together to the viceroy's.

Within two hundred yards of the Phoenix column the duo were set upon by men wielding 12-inch long surgical knives, Burke having been identified with the assistance of a Castle employee named Joe Smith. Initially, Joe Brady knelt down in their path apparently tying his bootlaces in a ruse to impede the pair's

Chief Secretary Lord Frederick Cavendish

A sketch of the murder scene outside the viceregal lodge
From the Illustrated London News, *May 1882*

progress. Springing forward, Brady lunged at Burke, knifing him in the back. Kelly attacked Cavendish stabbing him repeatedly while Cavendish tried vainly to fight him off while shouting for help from passersby. Finally, Brady cut Burke's throat and they and the others fled the scene in a cab driven by James 'skin the goat' Fitzharris.

Burke expired almost immediately and Cavendish was still breathing his last when two cyclists came on the scene to render assistance. Most onlookers perceived it to be a drunken brawl as did Earl Spencer who witnessed the scene from the windows of the viceregal lodge.

The Liffey was searched for the murder weapons up as far as Strawberry Beds. A cab had been seen exiting the Chapelizod gate at great speed. This was the meagre of evidence the police had to go on.

The political fall out was immediate causing immense embarrassment to the Land League, Parnell and the Irish Party in Westminister. Cavendish was married to Prime Minister Gladstone's niece Lucy and had been appointed by Gladstone as a goodwill emissary to Ireland. Ironically, the Invincibles did not realise that Burke's companion was Lord Cavendish. Their target was Burke firstly because he was Irish born and secondly a Roman Catholic (his mother was a sister of Cardinal Wiseman), and was, therefore, in their eyes, a betrayer of his country and his religion.

Eight months later Superintendent John Mallon of the Dublin Metropolitian police rounded up some twenty suspects who were tried for complicity in the crime. Superintendent Mallon tricked the Dublin leader of the Invincibles, James Carey, into informing by leading him to believe that Carey himself was being betrayed. The following were executed: Joe Brady, Michael Fagan, Patrick

*The Viceregal Lodge in 1783, from an engraving by Thomas Milton after a drawing
by J.J. Barralet.
Courtesy of Fingal County Council*

Delaney, Daniel Curley, Thomas Caffrey and Tim Kelly. All the hangings were carried out by Wiliam Marwood in Kilmainham Gaol. Marwood was paid a retainer of £20 per annum plus £10 for each execution. There was an added bonus whereby the hangman was allowed keep the deceased garments. They were usually sold to Madame Tussaud's gallery.

The knives had been smuggled into Dublin hidden in the skirts of the wife of Frank Byrne, Secretary of the Land League. They both escaped to America having been apparently tipped off by Carey. Carey himself was shot by Pat O'Donnell aboard the 'Melrose' bound for South Africa. O'Donnell was subsequently hanged in Newgate later that year.

Repercussions from these killings continued to reverberate with the Parnell forgery case as a direct consequence. As late as 1913 William Martin Murphy, among others, was suspected of putting out a false story that Jim Larkin the Labour Leader was the illegitimate son of Carey in an attempt to undermine him and his cause.

There was little public sympathy for the Invincibles. The killings were messy; knives were never a weapon of first choice for physical force Republicans. The victims were both unarmed. The events mired the Land League's and Parnell's efforts in the Irish Party and caused anti-Irish rioting in England. On the other hand, there was no time for Carey and other informers and to this day a 'carey'

James Carey

is Dublin slang for a spy or a traitor.

Lady Cavendish, in a gesture of true Christianity, sent Joe Brady an ivory crucifix to console him while he was awaiting execution. It is believed that this was purloined by Marwood the hangman.

Tim Kelly, the youngest of the assailants, told the prison chaplain that he could not and would not ever forgive Carey. The chaplain arranged for a nun, a Sister of Mercy, to visit Kelly and persuade him to purge his soul of this hatred before he would meet his Maker. Kelly asked the nun if she could forgive someone who would betray her or her friends and family in the fashion Carey did. The nun revealed to him that she was first cousin to Thomas H. Burke and, yes, she did forgive him and his fellow conspirators for the murder of her relative. They then knelt down to pray, Tim Kelly following the nun's example in forgiveness.

The night before his execution, the 21-year-old former chorister Kelly, from the privacy of his cell, sung in a fine clear voice various airs from *Maritana*. His finale was Wallace's beautiful song 'The Memory of the Past.' The visit from the nun obviously helped reconcile him to his fate, thus his ability to meet death singing.

One of those sentenced with the Invincibles was James Fitzharris, alias 'Skin-the-Goat'. He was the driver of the sidecar that transported the assassins. He was originally sent down for life but was later released.

ÁRAS AN UACHTARÁIN

Formerly the Viceregal Lodge and before that the Park Ranger's Lodge, this fine house was built in 1751 by Nathaniel Clements, a kinsman of the earls of Leitrim. The house was originally much smaller than it is now: it has been greatly – and gracefully– extended over the years.

The position of park ranger was a sinecure – a means of financially rewarding royal favourites. The real work of looking after the Park was delegated to subordinates. The government purchased the house in 1782 for about £10,000 for use as a viceregal residence but it was only used occasionally. After the Act of Union (1801), it was decided to make it more fit for the viceregal presence.

The earl of Hardwick had the wings added in about 1803, and in 1808 the duke of Richmond commissioned the fine Doric portico which was added to the north side. In 1816 the south portico, with its Ionic columns, was added by Francis Johnston, the architect who also designed the GPO. The last viceroy, Lord Fitzalan, bade farewell to Ireland in 1922 and thus ended British rule in twenty-six of Ireland's thirty-two counties.

The new post of governor-general was given to Tim Healy, a member of the old Irish Parliamentary Party and Parnell's most vocal critic during the split. He was followed into office by James McNeill and then by Donal Buckley, who was appointed by Eamonn De Valera when Fianna Fáil came to power. Buckley's brief was to do nothing and let the office wither away. The first president was Douglas Hyde; he was followed by Sean T. O'Kelly, Eamonn De Valera, Erskine Childers, Cearbhaill O'Dálaigh, Patrick Hillery, Mary Robinson and now Mary McAleese.

According to a humorous story doing the rounds at the time, during Healy's tenure of office he invited some senior army officers to dinner. The officers commanding the army at the time owed their rank from combat in the field and were not noted for their social finesse. During dinner Healy picked up a stick of celery and took a dainty bite. One officer supposedly nudged his neighbour at table and said, 'Would you look at oul' Tim eating the flowers!' Whether the story was designed to bring Tim down a peg or to discredit the officer corps is not apparent. The Áras hosted many receptions; recent guests have included numerous United States presidents and other heads of state.

A particularly fond memory I have is of John F. Kennedy's visit in June 1963, just before his tragic assassination. JFK's car stopped at the gates of the American ambassador's residence, across the road from the Áras, and he took time to shake hands with a crowd of local children, of which I was one.

The ambassador's residence, originally the chief secretary's residence, was built in 1776 by Sir John Blacquire – the 'king's cowboy' whom we met in an earlier chapter. The last occupant was Sir Hamar Greenwood, who was one of the chief apologists for the Black and Tans. The Americans took up residence here in 1927, the first envoy being Fredrick A. Stirling.

The Fifteen Acres (actually over 200 acres) was used for military displays and reviews and in more recent times for momentous religious gatherings. High Mass, attended by almost a million people, was celebrated here during the Eucharistic Congress in 1932. At this Mass the tenor John McCormack sang 'Panis Angelicus'. The 1,500-year-old bell of St Patrick was lent by the National Museum for the occasion and rang out for the first time in centuries.

This attendance was surpassed in 1979, when Pope John Paul celebrated mass at the spot now marked by a large papal cross. During his visit the streets were decked with flags and there was great excitement. The anticlimax when the visit ended was described by one wag as 'post-papal depression'. In times gone by this area was known as a duelling ground; ironically, many of those engaged in this illegal practice were members of the legal profession.

Nearer to the Castleknock end of the park is the Ordnance Survey building, previously Mountjoy Cavalry Barracks. Before that it was home to Luke Gardiner, who built his residence here in 1725–26 using some of the stone from Castleknock Castle. His grandson, Luke Gardiner, Lord Mountjoy, was killed while fighting the Wexford insurgents during the battle of New Ross in 1798. He had been a member of the Irish Volunteers and commanded the Castleknock Cavalry. The names of Gardiner Street and Place and Mountjoy Square commemorate his name. Luke Gardiner was associated with the building and layout of this part of the city, which features Georgian squares and broad avenues. Such was his interest in the theatre that he included one in his residence. In 1812 the house and lands were given over for use as a cavalry barracks and thirteen years later the property became the headquarters of the Ordnance Survey, for which purpose it is still in use today.

Further down we reach the Furry Glen (possibly a corruption of 'furzey', from the furze (Ulex) bushes that would have grown along the glenside before the park was tamed). There is a little spring (Baker's Well), obscured by a small hillock, to the left of the road heading toward Knockmaroon Gate. This spring feeds the Furry Glen Lake; this is perhaps the most beautiful part of the park and has for long been a traditional courting spot. There is a tradition that the area around the lake is haunted by the ghost of a policeman who appears during a full moon. The edge of the Fifteen Acres overlooking the Furry Glen has been a venue for model-aeroplane flying and on Sunday mornings it is a sight to behold, with miniature aircraft looping the loop and performing stupendous aeronautical feats.

Close by is St Mary's Hospital, formerly the Hibernian Military School, built between 1766 and 1768 for the orphans and children of soldiers in Ireland. The chapel attached to the school was where the viceroy attended Sunday worship. It was built in 1773. One of the chaplains, the Rev. Peter Le Fanu, was the father of the author Joseph Sheridan Le Fanu. The girls were transferred to the Drummond School in Chapelizod in the mid-1860s. Both schools ceased to function when the British army left in 1922. The Royal Infirmary nearby, also part of the hospital complex was built between 1786 and1788. The present St Mary's Hospital was renowned for its success in treating tuberculosis. Close by is the dolmen or tumulus at Knockmary Hill. Skeletons, pottery and sea-shells forming a necklace and an arrowhead were found when it was opened in 1838. Another dolmen, closer to Chapelizod, was removed to Dublin Zoo and re-erected there.

Continuing on to Thomas Hill, the visitor will reach the Magazine Fort, which was built in 1735 on the site of the old Phoenix manor house. Some authorities give 1801 as the year of construction and quote Dean Swift's verse on seeing it. Swift died in 1745, however, so the date of 1801 must be to do with some completion works. A print dated 1795 shows the building not un-like the structure that is there today. Swift had a healthy disrespect for govern-ment hierarchy and any form of authority. When the plans for the magazine were first mooted, the British parliament was actively depressing Irish trade and commerce and the Irish economy was in a desperate state. So Swift penned the following squib:

> Behold! a proof of Irish sense!
> Here Irish wit is seen!
> When nothing's left, that's worth defence,
> We build a magazine.

A party of Irish Volunteers in 1916, togged out as if for football, requested per-mission to 'get their ball back' and in doing so seized the fort and relieved the garrison of their rifles. They did not succeed in breaking into the fort proper, and the charges they laid failed to detonate. The raid was led by one Gary Holohan, who had actually worked in the fort.

Just before Christmas 1939, the IRA visited the Magazine Fort on a similar errand. That an underground army could assemble thirteen lorries to remove almost every round of ammunition, together with rifles and machine-guns, without the police hearing was amazing – particularly on the eve of the Second World War, when the authorities should have been particularly vigilant. By the end of the month most of the materials had been recovered and over a hundred IRA members arrested. Was it a spectacular trap? Did the police have advance warning and allow it to go ahead as a good reason for rounding up known IRA members?

The Phoenix House that originally graced St Thomas Hill was built by Sir Edmund Fisher in 1611 on land leased from Sir Richard Sutton, who had in turn been granted it by King James I, against the advice of Sir Arthur Chichester, lord deputy (an ancestor of the late Capt. Terence O'Neill and Major Chichester-Clark, both former Stormont premiers). Six years later the incoming lord deputy, Sir Oliver St John, took the lands back for the crown for use as a viceregal residence and awarded Sir Edward Fisher £2,500 in lieu. St John occupied the house, having made some alterations and extensions. He was later raised to the peerage as Lord Grandison. He was replaced by Lord Falkland and then by the earl of Stafford.

Lord Ranelagh lived in the house for a while but was not happy with the hunting opportunities it afforded, and the duke of Ormonde possibly never got time to use the house, as the times were so troubled. The outskirts of the city would have caused security problems. General Charles Fleetwood, the 'Chief Governor', and his wife, Bridget Cromwell (Oliver's daughter), lived there, followed by Henry Cromwell, who became lord deputy. Fleetwood, like his father-in-law, was a 'dyed-in-the-wool' tyrant; Henry, however, was of a milder and more tolerant disposition, according to accounts of the period. Lord Ormonde, on his second time around, finally got to live there, and commenced the work, referred to earlier, that gave us our Phoenix Park.

An article in the *Freeman's Journal* after Phoenix Park became a people's park in 1770 is wonderfully descriptive. It reads: 'Under the rule of Mr Clements every impropriety was rigorously expelled from that beautiful spot. Ill-looking strollers of either sex could never get admittance at the gate except on public occasions. Cars and noddies (the cheapest form of shay – a two wheeled

carriage for one or two usually drawn by one horse between shafts) were refused passage. But now the gates are opened wide to Tag, Rag and Bobtail.
The sabbath is abused by permitting a hurling match to be played there every
Sunday evening which is productive of blasphemous speaking, riot, drunkenness, broken heads, dislocated bones, among the thousand of the lower class:
and meanwhile the deer are hunted by detached parties of these vagrants and
their dogs'.

The beautiful gas lamps that were once lit individually by a lamplighter, who
did his rounds on his bike, are often commented on. They were installed by the
Hibernian Gas Co., in 1859 and fully refurbished in 1987.

During the Second World War turf was stored in the Fifteen Acres and the
remains of the banks could be seen on the side of the road for years afterwards,
giving great entertainment to children as places for climbing and jumping. In
the early 1950s there was a big newspaper story of a leprechaun's corpse having
been discovered in the park. Some quite sober commentators took it more seriously than one would have expected, and crowds gathered from far and wide to
see the 'corpse'. It proved to be a large, gnarled fungus.

The North Circular Road gate lodge was the meeting place where Bohemi-
ans Football Club was founded on September 9 1890. There were two cricket
clubs in Phoenix Park; Phoenix Cricket Club was founded in 1863. There were
upward of 20 cricket grounds in the Phoenix Park in the early 1900s. Polo has
been played in the Phoenix Park at the 'nine acres' since 1874 and is usually
played on Saturday evening and is very exciting to watch.

8

CHAPELIZOD

The old pub yarn goes that this village got its name when King Sitric, the leader of the Danes, was galloping across the Fifteen Acres when he saw the church down below and said to his companion, 'What chapel is it'? It has been suggested that the village, which was once a walled town, got its name from Isolde, an Irish princess. Isolde loved Tristan, the champion of King Mark of Cornwall, who killed Sir Marlin, brother of the queen of Ireland. When Tristan arrived in the Irish court, the queen observed that his sword was missing a piece, which matched exactly a piece she had extracted from her brother's body. He was banished and Isolde followed him. The two were buried side by side. A tree grew from each plot and the branches of the two embraced. Thus the lovers became joined in death.

One authority, the late President Douglas Hyde, however, suggests the name 'Chapelizod' came from Séipéal Easóige ('stoat's chapel'), while John O'Donovan (1809–61), a scholar of equal merit, comes down in favour of *Séipéal Íseal* (low-lying chapel'). The derivation from 'Isolde' is lovely, linking as it does with the Arthurian legends of Tristan and Isolde, but the 'chapel of the weasel or stoat' explanation seems unlikely. The last, however, *Séipéal Íseal*, is an exact description of the area, surrounded as it is by hills. Officialdom seems to go with the Isolde theory, but your choice, whatever it may be, has as much going for it as their explanation. The locals, for years, pronounced 'Chapelizod' as 'Chapel Lizard', and the Down Survey calls it 'Chappellizzard'. The village formed part of Hugh Tyrell's land following the Norman invasion. Tyrell later transferred it to The Knight Hospitallers of St John of Jerusalem. Many Norman knights owed a debt to this religious military order, which tended the knights' wounds sustained while on crusade. The crown appears to have reclaimed the estate in 1478 and vested it in Sir Thomas Daniel. Part of Chapelizod had been granted to the De La Felde family in 1200, but this area seemed

Chapelizod in the early 1900s. The four storey building in the background was where James Joyce's father worked.
Photograph from the Lawrence collection, courtesy of the National Library of Ireland.

to be absorbed by the Knights. Following Henry VIII's break with Rome, the monastic lands of this area were seized by the crown.

Sir Henry Power (later Lord Valentia), an Elizabethan adventurer, was granted the manor of Chapelizod for services rendered to the earl of Essex while in Ireland. He had commanded the army in Munster in 1598 and represented Queen's County in parliament in 1613, besides being a member of the privy council. Before his Irish adventures he had sailed with Sir Francis Drake in the Caribbean.

The famous poet and lawyer Sir John Davies (1565–1618) lived in Chapelizod at this time. It was he who rode to inform James IV of Scotland of Queen Elizabeth's death, which made the Scottish monarch James I of England. Sir John held the title of Irish attorney general and speaker. He was appointed lord chief justice of England but died before taking office. He was also a founder of the Society of Antiquaries.

PORTER'S GUIDE AND DIRECTORY FOR CHAPELIZOD 1912

Chapelizod is an interesting village three miles south of the General Post Office, Dublin. It is pleasantly situation on the banks of the River Liffey, principally in the barony of Castleknock, comprising about 60 acres, with a population of 1,250. The chief industry in the neighbourhood is the Phoenix Park Distillery, which gives employment to a considerable number of hands. It is one of the few distilleries in Ireland that is gradually increasing its output, notwithstanding the delicate attentions of Mr Lloyd George.

Before the erection of the viceregal lodge it was the residence of the viceroy and not unlikely to become in the immediate future the residence of a lord chancellor of Ireland. The principal buildings are the Church of Ireland – a venerable pile covered with ivy – attached to which there is a massive tower in the old baronial style. The Catholic church is a handsome and capacious structure capable of accommodating 800 worshippers. There are very large Convent Boarding and Day schools at Mount Sackville, where upwards of 100 children receive a high-class education. There are the Boys' National Schools, a very fine new building, with an average attendance of nearly 200, under the capable control of Mr James Reidy, and a Girls' School under the charge of Mrs O'Donovan. The Drummond Institute at Mulberry Hill provides a comfortable home, clothing and education for the orphan daughters of soldiers. It is under the management of Miss Rouselle, and is regarded as one of the most successful institutions of the kingdom. There is a Postal and Money Order Office, RIC Barracks and Dispensary.

Catholic Church: Rev. J.P. McSwiggan, PP; Rev. E. O'Reilly, CC; Rev. J. Cahill,C.C.

Church of Ireland: Rev. A.D. Purefoy, Incumbent, The Rectory.

St Joseph's Convent, Mount Sackville – Board and Day School.

Chapelizod Boys' National Schools – James Reidy, Principal.

Chapelizod Girls' National Schools – Mrs O'Donovan, Principal.

Drummond Institute for the Orphan Daughters of Soldiers, Mulberry Hill – MissRouselle, Lady Superintendent.

Anderson, J., Relieving Officer.

Chapelizod Dispensary – Dr McMahon, Medical Officer.

RIC Barracks – Segt. O'Donovan in charge.

CHAPELIZOD RESIDENTS

(A) Andrews, J., 4, Hibernian Terrace. (B) Baron, Thomas, Knockmary Lodge. Bearman, H.T., Annamore, Ballyfermot. Blakemore, Elizabeth, Clayton Terrace. Blight, E. Phoenix Villa. Bowie, Mrs, King's Terrace. Bracken, J. Provision Dealer. Brannigan, T. Brett, T., Inland Revenue. Broadbent, Mrs R., Glenthorn House. Byrne, Patrick, Farmer, Gallanstown. (C) Cahill, Rev. J., Caird, Mrs Hill View. Cant, David. Cant, George, Cardiff House. Cant., Wm., P., St Laurence's Lodge. Capon, Mrs Sabine Terrace. Carroll, Mrs Chapelizod Lodge. Caulfield, Laurence, Grocer and Spirit Merchant. Collins, F.T., Mount Ida. Conroy, Daniel, Chapelizod Road. Corbally, Mrs Font Hill. (D) Dalton, Mrs Garden Vale. Davis, J. Sergt., D.M.P. Darling, Mrs Rivermount. De Sales, Mrs Springvale. Delny, Mrs Mary, The Orchard. Dockeray, DR, Culmore. Donnelly, M., Park View Terrace. Dowling, P. Farmer, Gallanstown. Doyle, M.J., Grocer and Vintner, Strawberry Beds. Drummond Institure for the Orphan Daughters of Soldiers, Mulberry Hill, Miss Rouselle, Matron. Duffy, A., Quarryfield. Dunbar, T., Builder, St Mary's Terrace. Dunmore, E., Clayton Terrace. (E) Eager, Mr, Liffey Vale. Egan, D.J., Dale View. Elliott, Mrs M., Stonehouse, Ballyfermott. Ennis, Mrs Mary, Vintner, Strawberry Beds. Evers, R., Park Terrace. (F) Fahy, Mr, Riverside House. Fitzpatrick, Mrs M., Coal, Stationery, Newsagent, Post Office. Finnigan, Mrs E., Provision Dealer. Flynn, Mrs Mardyke Mills. Fortin, Robert, General Manager, White House, Ballyfermott. (G) Garland, D., J.P., Cromville. Geraghty, P., Ballyfermott Cottage. Gill, J., Liffey Vale. Gilman, Wm. G., Wine and Spirit Merchant, Carisle Terrace. Ging, Christopher, Grover and Vintner, The Bridge Inn and The Old Kildare. Godden, George, Riverside House. Guinness, The Hon. Arthur E., Glenmaroon. (H) Halpin, Thomas, Vintner, Phoenix Tavern. Hands, George, Martin's Row. Harmsworth, Mr, Sunnybank. Healy, Timothy, M.P., K.C., Glenauldin. Henderson, Selina, 2, Hibernian Terrace. Hobson, Mrs Leburnham Cottage. Hogan, T., St Mary's

Terrace. Hutchings, Richard, Park View Terrace. (J) Johns, Mrs, 5, Hibernian Terrace. (K) Kelly, Timothy, Hibernian House. Keys, Mrs Margaret, Wine and Spirit Merchant, The Mullingar House. (L) Lawlor, Patrick, Farmer, Ballyfermott. (M) Mackey, Mrs E., Orchard Lodge. McAllen, Henry, Clayton Terrace. McKenzie, John, Ordnance Survey. McMahon, Dr A.P., Medical Officer, The Dispensary. McMahon, John, Gardenville. McMahon, Wm., Mayfield House. McSwiggan, Rev. J.P., P.P., The Presbytery. McWhirter, J.W., Tailor, Garden Lodge. Mangan, Mrs M. Quarry Vale. Malley, George A., Sunnyrise. Markey, George, Desmond House. Maycock, Elizabeth, Sabine Terrace. Morrissey, T., Chapelizod House. Murphy, Mrs A., St Laurence. Murray, James, Vintner, Ballyfermott Bridge. (N) Nicholson, J., Manager, Phoenix Park Distillery. Nolan, Michael, Wheelwright, St Laurence. (O) O'Connor Bros. Victuallers. O'Donohoe, D.J., Clayton Terrace. O'Meara, Christopher, Carpenter, The Bridge, Ballyfermott. O'Reilly, Rev. E., c.c., Hibernian Terrace. (P) Palmer, Mrs Hill View. Palmer, Ernest, Registrar of Titles. Peat, Mrs M., General Warehouse. Phoenix Park Distillery, J. Nicholson, Manager. Powell, George, Glenburnie Purefoy, The Rev. Amyrald, Church of Ireland, The Rectory. (R) Rea, John, Boundary Villa. Reidy, James, Headmaster, Chapelizod National Schools. Rourke, J. Phoenix Villa. (S) Saunders, Miss Mary, New Holland Iron Mills. Saville, Wm. J., Clayton Terrace. Scully, Mrs Strawberry Beds. Sheridan, J., 3, Hibernian Terrace. Smyth, P., D.M.P. Spendlow, Mrs Sarah, Belgrove Dairy. Spring, Mrs, Johnstown House. (T) Thompson, Mrs Tierney, Luke, Gravel Quarry. Tubb, Francis. (V) Vincent, John, Glenmaroon Cottage. (W) Walker, Mrs B., Vintner, Kildare Inn. Walters, M. L.R.C.P.S.I., Medical Officer for Chapelizod. White, J., Glenville. White, Mrs, Sabine Terrace. Williams, Mrs Vintner and Restaurant, Strawberry Hall. Williamson, Wm., Clayton Terrace. Willoughby, J., Glenmaroon, Park Gate.

THE KING'S HOUSE

Lord Valentia had his house built where the industrial estate is today, an area which was once used for greyhound racing as Chapelizod dog track. By all accounts, Valentia's house was an imposing structure with fifteen chimneys. It was occupied by William III for a period after the Battle of the Boyne. Following that, Sir Theophilus Jones, the brother of Col Michael Jones, commander of the parliamentary forces, lived there. On Ormonde's return to power after the Restoration, it was granted to Sir Maurice Eustace, then recently appointed lord chancellor of Ireland. Sir Maurice was a Hebrew scholar and a member of the legal profession. He had previously been imprisoned for seven years because of his royalist sympathies. Ormonde at this time had started to enclose the park, and Eustace allowed 400 acres of it to be sold for inclusion.

The redoubtable Dodson, the jerry-builder of the park's walls, was engaged to refurbish the 'King's House' in Chapelizod for use as a residence for the viceroy and to rebuild the bridge over the Liffey there. The house was another botched job, but the bridge survived. Some time in the 1670s a Col Richard Lawrence, encouraged by Ormonde, set up a new industry for the manufacture of linen and other textiles, including woollen goods. He brought in Hugenot French workers from La Rochelle and Ile de Ré (off the coast of La Rochelle) and, with army contracts, kept the enterprise going for several years. Following this, the Lovett family ran the business. Christopher Lovett became lord mayor of Dublin. His wife was a descendant of Rory O'Moore, her sister was the wife of the religious reformer John Knox and her grandson was Edward Lovett Pearce, the architect who designed the Houses of Parliament, later the Bank of Ireland in College Green.

WHISKY AND LITERATURE

The woollen business continued but was in steep decline. The linen business, however, thrived, with a linen mill operated by a Mr Crosthwaite employing several hundred. Crowthwaite was generous in financially assisting the education of local children. William Dargan (of railway fame) opened a mill for spinning linen thread from locally grown flax. This thread achieved a top award at the Paris Exhibition of 1855. The linen industry went north and the factory was sold to the Distillers Company of Edinburgh in 1878. The Distillers Company made Scotch whisky for export and later traded as the Phoenix Distillery and the Dublin and Chapelizod Distillery Company; James Joyce's father was secretary there for a time. There was a huge fire in the Chapelizod distillery in 1901, but production recommenced. The main customer was the British War Office, which required drink for consumption in various army and navy posts throughout the British Empire. Business tapered off after Irish independence and the distillery closed shortly after.

Joseph Sheridan Le Fanu
Painting by Brindsley Le Fanu, courtesy of
the National Gallery of Ireland

Brunswick of Ireland later acquired the premises with a view to the manufacturing of bowling alleys for export. Telecom Éireann subsequently used the property as a depot and it is now the site of luxury apartments. Joyce referred to it as 'the still that was a mill' in *Finnegan's Wake*. The tavern-keeper H.C. Earwicker is identified with the Mullingar House. In *A Portrait of the Artist as a Young Man*, Stephen Dedalus describes his father as 'a medical student, an oarsman, a tenor, an amateur actor, a shouting politician, a small landlord, a small investor, a drinker, a good fellow, a storyteller, somebody's secretary, something in a distillery, a tax gatherer, a bankrupt and at present a praiser of his own past.'

The Temple family were landlords of Chapelizod, and Sir John Temple was raised to the peerage as Lord Palmerston. A member of this distinguished family, Henry John Temple, Third Viscount Palmerston, was Prime Minister of Britain for two terms in 1855–58 and again in 1859–65. Nearly two centuries earlier, Sir William Temple (1628–99) had been patron to Dean Swift; while residing with him, Swift met Stella, daughter of Sir William's housekeeper. It was rumoured at the time that Swift was Temple's natural son and Stella was

Temple's natural daughter, which would have made them step-siblings. Another variant of the story is that Swift was the natural grandson of Sir William and therefore Stella's step-nephew.

The 'King's House', having become unfit for human habitation, was given over for use as an artillery barracks in about 1760. The horses stabled here produced a huge quantity of a substance that gave the name 'Midden Row', which has since been politely changed to 'Maiden Row'. The soldiers had plenty of scope for quenching their thirst at such premises as the Salmon House, the Three Tuns and Grapes, the Ship Tavern and the Mullingar House, which were all open for business in Chapelizod.

Lord Northcliffe, the newspaper magnate, responsible for the *Daily Mail*, *Daily Mirror* and *Evening News*, was a native of Chapelizod. He was born here in 1865 as Alfred Charles Harmsworth. His father taught in the Hibernian School and Alfred was born in a house called Sunnybank on Knockmaroon Hill. His watchword to his journalists was 'Explain; simplify; clarify'. He acquired control of the *Times* in 1908, having earlier saved the *Observer* from extinction. His brothers, Alfred Harold and Cecil Bishop, became respectively Viscount Rothermere and Baron Harmsworth. Another brother, Robert, became a baronet – not bad from a family of fourteen children.

St Laurence, on the south side of the Liffey, was deemed to be a separate village. It took its name from a house for lepers dedicated to St Laurence. Its previous name was *Tigh Guaire* ('Guaire's house'). The name Guaire means proud or generous and was a common name in early Christian Ireland. The Norsemen changed the name to 'Stagori'. The film *This Other Eden* was shot in Chapelizod, as was the 1930 film *Song O' My Heart*, featuring John McCormack.

Joseph Sheridan Le Fanu (1814–73), whose father was chaplain at the Hibernian School, was also to make his name in the field of journalism, having eschewed a legal career. He owned the *Evening Mail*, the *Warden*, the *Dublin Evening Packet* and the *Dublin University Magazine*. He wrote *Uncle Silas* (1864); *The House By The Churchyard* (1863) a thriller set in Chapelizod; and the vampire tale *Carmilla* (1872). Bram Stoker (1847–1911), the Dublin-born author of *Dracula* (1897), worked for the *Evening Mail,* and Le Fanu's works were to lend him the ideas that resulted in his great gothic horror tale.

An interesting story is related by Le Fanu about his mother. She was a regular visitor to Major Sirr's residence in North Great George's Street. It was Sirr who arrested the patriot Lord Edward Fitzgerald before the 1798 Rising. (He also apprehended Robert Emmet.) During the mêlée, Lord Edward sustained wounds from which he died. The dagger he used to defend himself was taken by Sirr and displayed in his house. Le Fanu's mother formed the opinion that it should not be in Sirr's possession and removed it surreptitiously while on a visit. Her family thus became custodians of this historic dagger. It is often speculated that the large old house beside the Anglican church is the house in his Chapelizod novel. The church dates back to the 1300s. In the year 1740 Dr Stone, the bishop of Ossory, was consecrated here. The present structure was built in 1832. An interesting epitaph on the tomb of Sir Richard Wilcox reads: 'Praises on the tombs are trifles idly spent; a man's good name is his own monument'.

In 1843 the foundation stone of the church of the Nativity of the Blessed Virgin Mary was laid. The new church was consecrated on 3 June 1849 by Archbishop Murray. Fr Dungan was parish priest of Blanchardstown at the time, and this Chapelizod church served as a chapel-of-ease until it became temporarily a separate parish in 1883; it was made permanent in 1897. The church was built at the height of the Famine. One can imagine the efforts required to raise funds; indeed a significant amount of money was collected in Liverpool. There was a famine-relief committee in Chapelizod; the lord lieutenant subscribed £171 to it in January 1847. Another famous resident was Tim Healy, who did more than anyone else to bring down Parnell following the revelation of his liaison with Catherine (Kitty) O'Shea. He lived in a house called Glenaulin; later he was to become Ireland's first governor-general.

9

KNOCKMAROON AND GLENMAROON

These place names have been interpreted as 'the hill' and 'the valley of the secret', but some authorities suggest that the name of both came from that of St Maolruain of Tallaght. Indeed there was a pattern held in Tallaght called Moll Rooney's fair, an obvious corruption of St Maolruain. Our knowledge of this saint is so scant that we do not even know if the holy one was a man or a woman.

The Sisters of Charity run a school there for girls with special needs in their convent of the Holy Angels and also look after girls in St Vincent's on the Navan Road, Ashtown. The property was previously owned by Hon. Arthur Guinness and before that by Alexander Ferrier of Ferrier Pollock & Co. The firm of Ferrier Pollock traded in textiles and operated from Powerscourt House in South William Street, now the Powerscourt Centre.

There is a slightly risqué tale concerning the late Brendan Behan and some students worth relating. Brendan Behan was fond of drinking in McDaids of Harry Street, actually he was fond of drinking anywhere. One day the story goes he was holding court with a few of his drinking cronies, when a group of Trinity students entered the pub. One of the group spotted Behan and thought, incorrectly as it turned out, that he would have a bit of sport out of our slightly tipsy hero. 'Mr Behan,' intoned the student in a swanky 'Rathgar' accent, 'I wonder if you could describe to us poor students the difference between prose and poetry.' Quick as a light, Behan said 'I will,' and this is what he said:

> There was a young man named Timothy Brand,
> Who worked for Ferrier Pollocks,
> One day while out on Sandymount Strand,
> The tide came up to his knee.

'That's prose, lads,' said Behan 'but if there was a high tide that day it would have been poetry.' Brendan 1 – Students 0. The story could be apocryphal, but it's a good yarn!

Col H.T. Colby, who conducted the Ordnance Survey of the entire country in 1825, lived here for a while. He was so interested in his task that it is said he drew no salary. The excellence and accuracy of his work holds to this day. There is a freshwater spring in the grounds that is remarkable for the purity of its water. There was a strong opinion that there were coal-bearing seams in the locality, and five deep shafts were sunk in this area of Knockmaroon Hill – but to no avail.

The Convent of the Sisters of St Joseph of Cluny bought Mt Sackville in 1864 from Lieutenant Col Henry Holden. The Sisters were originally based in Blanchardstown but their premises there were not suitable for use as a girls school. This order came from France at the invitation of Dr Cullen, archbishop of Dublin following a suggestion from Fr Lemon of the Holy Ghost Fathers. His order previously ran the Blanchardstown seminary before moving to Blackrock. Their Rev. Mother was Calixte Pichet, and the purchase price of the property was £8,750. Mr J. Hawkins lived in Mt Sackville in 1837, according to Samuel Lewis' *Topographical Dictionary of Ireland* (1837), and before that Lord George Sackville, who acted as his father's chief secretary when he was viceroy and was then park ranger in 1761, resided there. Sackville had a very mixed career, as he was disgraced as a result of failure to carry out orders at Minden in 1759 during the Seven Years War. He had previously fought well in 1745 at Fontenoy, where he advanced deep into French lines, was wounded and taken prisoner. As colonial secretary, his poor coordination of operations led to the surrender of General Burgoyne to the Americans at the Battle of Saratoga in 1777. He changed his name to 'Germain' when he was left a fortune by a wealthy heiress of that name.

FARMLEIGH

The Guinness estate of Farmleigh, formerly owned by Lord Iveagh, is famed for its beauty and its clock tower, which is visible for miles around. The tower

Farmleigh in 1873
Courtesy of Fingal County Council

The Clock Tower, Farmleigh
Photograph by Brendan Campion

was built between 1870 and 1880 of limestone quarried from across the Liffey at Palmerstown. The dressing, balcony supports and stairs are of granite. The tower is 200 feet high and the thickness of the walls tapers from 4 feet at the base to 2.5 feet at the top. About 140 feet up the tower, a door gives access to a balcony with magnificent views in all directions. The tower is really a water tower, holding 1,800 gallons of water raised from the Liffey near Mill Lane, Palmerstown, 80 feet below the building's base. The clock mechanism was installed by Sir Howard Grubb, the maker of astronomical instrument.

The principal stonemason working on the tower was Patrick Connolly, helped by local craftsmen James Campell, Patrick Murray and John Finnegan. The gravel and sand were supplied by Mr Treacy of the Lower Road. Mr Wilson of Guinness' brewery was clerk of works. In 1837 Charles French lived at Farmley (sic), followed by William English, Mrs Ferrar and J.C. Coote. Edward Cecil Guinness bought the building in 1873. The house and estate were acquired from the Guinness family in June 1999 for government use. It is used for entertaining foreign heads of state and dignitaries and also on occasions for accommodating these guests on their visits. It is open to the public during most weekends and has become a mecca for lovers of music in summer when it hosts open-air concerts.

James O'Driscoll, in his excellent book *Cnucha* suggests that the name 'Farm-ley' (the original spelling) is a reference to the 'castle farme of Castleknock', to differentiate it from the northern portion of the townland, the 'Churchtowne of Castleknock' as described in the 1659 census. Lord Iveagh had previously allowed the government to use the house for entertaining European Union ministers.

'YOU TAKE THE HIGH ROAD … '

The castellated house called Castlemount was originally owned by a German family called Koenig ('king' in English). The family named the house 'Schloss-berg', literally 'Castleknock', if you accept the 'knock' as meaning 'hill' or 'mount'. The German word Schloss ('castle') and Berg ('mountain') combine to give the name 'Schlossberg'.

The Guinness residence of Knockmaroon House was originally the property of Henry Warren Darley; owners included Sir Henry Marsh, Walter Stephen Brinkley and his son Capt. John Turner Brinkley. When Lord Moyne first appeared in the House of Lords, the yarn goes, one earl nudged his neighbour, saying, 'Who's 'e then?' and the reply was, 'Oh, Moyne's a Guinness'.

On the high road to Lucan via Porterstown (the lower road being along the Liffey) may be seen the Sandpit Cottages at Diswellstown, with their distinctive blue and white colours. The cottages were built for the tenants of the Guinness estate. One of the last of the true bards – Thomas Bracken – resided here. Tommy wrote poems about sporting events, political stories and indeed anything newsworthy. No sooner did something of significance happen then Tommy would be up and about selling copies of his latest ballad. He was a tremendously popular figure, but unfortunately he is no longer with us. Tommy died in November 1991 at the relatively young age of forty-eight. Those whom the gods love die young. Tommy would exchange ideas on poetry with the late

Lord Moyne, a significant poet himself, who died in 1992. I reproduce here a poem in Tommy's own hand about his native place; the poem was given to me by his sister Katie:

Castleknock

Castleknock is my native place;
Your woods and fields abound in me.
Though progress tends to change your face
It cannot erase my memories.
I see you on a summer's day,
Fields of green and new mown hay,
Cattle grazing, rabbits racing,
Hawthorn hedges along the way,
Primroses growing along the ditches
Add to my priceless riches.
Fond playground of my childhood days,
Woodlands, hillocks, fields and maize
Please claim me when death has its say
So that I'll rest within your clay.

The Bracken family were related to Thomas Bracken, the man who wrote the national anthem of New Zealand. He was born on 21 December 1843 near Clonee, County Meath and wrote many poems after he emigrated to Australia and subsequently New Zealand. Someone in County Monaghan picked up his birthplace as Clones instead of Clonee, which resulted in the erection of a plaque on a public building in Clones celebrating Bracken's birth. If Tommy was alive no doubt he would have a poem about this. The Bracken family have distinguished themselves as generous benefactors of St Francis Hospice, Abbotstown.

Another local resident who brought his expertise to the arts was Cathal Gannon who made harpsichords.

Across the road from the Sandpit Cottages is the lovely walk down to the Liffey through the Glen. The Glen was quarried by Harris' about forty years ago for sand. Nature has reclaimed it and it is now a delightful leafy glen with a small stream tumbling down through it. Some locals say it is called the River Dis. The Deuswell family, who purchased 578 acres of land from Baron Tyrell in the thirteenth century, gave their name to Diswellstown. On the other hand, they may have taken their name from the Ragwell which was there. Was this holy well – Deus Well – God's Well? It was common enough for people to take their surnames from the locality in which they lived. The Ragwell was supposed to have a cure for the eyes. The thornbush associated with the well was burnt accidentally by travellers who lit a fire, apparently for cooking purposes, many years ago. The well now has a metal cover, over which has been laid a flowerbed. This spot is particularly beautiful in spring, when primroses greet the new season with their bright vibrant hues.

Oatlands House and grounds are on Porterstown Road just past the Sandpit Cottages and the Ragwell, but on the opposiite side of the road. Castleknock Hurling and Football Club are developing their new grounds next to Oatlands.

In times past, Oatlands was home to the Godley family in 1837. One of the Godley family served as a vicar in St Brigid's from 1764–1767. The Koenig family from Germany, who later moved to Castlemount (or Schloss Berg as they called it), resided there in 1914 and later in the 1940s, John A. Nicholson

The Sandpit Cottages
Painting by Fr Eugene Kennedy

Col. Chamberlain

lived there. Other occupants included members of the Guinness family. However, one of the most interesting occupants was Col Sir Neville Francis Fitzgerald Chamberlain, KCB, Inspector General of the Royal Irish Constabulary, who lived there from 1900 to 1916.

Col Chamberlain was a distant relative of the Chamberlain family that numbered among its members Neville Chamberlain, who was prime minister of Britain at the commencement of hostilities which resulted in the Second World War. He had previously followed a policy of appeasement that resulted in the Munich agreement, which failed to satisfy Herr Hitler's appetite for other nations territory.

Col Chamberlain was Inspector General of the RIC during the 1916 Rising and curiously ignored reports from British naval intelligence and other sources about the impending insurrection, leaving the RIC and British military totally unprepared for what happened.

Most of the British high command in Ireland was off at the Fairyhouse Races on Easter Monday when the Rising began and so 'the second city of the Empire' was in the hands of the rebels for one week. He was relieved of his office in August of that year and retired to hunting, shooting and fishing until his death in 1944. However, in his earlier life while with the 11th Devon Regiment serving in India, he invented the game of snooker. As a young subaltern posted in Jubbulpore between 1874 and 1876, he played a lot of billiards, which was a popular pastime with most young officers at the time. It appears that Jubbulpore was a quiet station and with time on his hands the young Chamberlain devised the game as an alternative to billiards.

Chamberlain's service in India became a little more active and slightly more perilous. He was wounded in the Afghan war while serving with the Central Indian Force. He remained there on his recovery, participating in the

Burmah Campaign and later on embarking to South Africa where he was private secretary to Lord Roberts during the Boer War.

Ironically, one of the houses he lived in during his early period in Dublin was the Hermitage in Rathfarnham, later home to Patrick Pearse – the main architect of the 1916 Rising which resulted in Chamberlain's downfall. While living there Chamberlain added a room to the house. It was, of course, a billiard room.

The junction at Somerton Lane was known as the 'Woolly Corner' locally as it was here that sheep were herded before being taken to market. The path at the right hand running to the side of Diswellstown House is known as 'Canon's Lane', supposedly because the canon used it as a short cut to Castleknock for parochial visitation. The Kennan family lived in this house for years, however, and the correct name for the path is more probably the similarly pronounced Kennan's Lane.

SOMERTON

Somerton, nearby, was home to the Brooke family. Two members of the Brooke family blazed a fiery trail in America. By August of 1812 the war between Britain and America was in its third year when a British force under Admiral Cockburn attacked Washington. Cols Arthur and Francis Brooke were leading a military raiding party and on entering an abandoned White House were delighted to come upon tables laden down with sumptuous food in preparation for a banquet. The president of the United States, James Madison, had vacated the house in some haste the previous evening.

The Brooke brothers and entourage tucked into the food and returned the hospitality of their unwitting host by torching the building. The White House was badly burned, only a torrential rainstorm spared the building from complete destruction. The architect, James Hoban, a native of Callan, County Kilkenny, had the building completely renovated later, during which time the grey stonework was painted white to cover up the scorch marks – hence the

'White House'. Hoban's original design for the White House was influenced by Richard Cassell's Leinster House. The Rotunda Hospital was also based on Leinster House.

The two firebrands involved were members of the Brooke family who lived in Summerton House overlooking the Strawberry Beds. The family settled here in the early 1800s having purchased the estate from a Councillor Dunne, he in turn had purchased it from Henry Lawes Luttrell, Lord Carhampton, in 1808. The lands on this portion of Luttrellstown estate were named Summerton after the village of the same name in Somerset owned by the senior branch of the Luttrell family. The Brookes were descended from Capt. Basil Brooke 1567–1633, who was awarded lands in Donegal for military service to the crown. His descendants later transferred to Colebrook, County Fermanagh, having been awarded the lands of the McMahon and Maguire clans, which had been forfeited by the crown. This family would later include Sir Basil Brooke, one time premier of Northern Ireland, and his brother Field Marshal Viscount Alan Brooke, foremost military advisor to Churchill during the Second World War.

The southern Brookes derived their fortune from land, banking and latterly the wine trade while continuing on a strong tradition of military service to the crown.

Raymond Francis Brooke was a grand master of the Order of Free Masons and was the author of *The Brimming River*, which describes life growing up in Summerton in the early years of the twentieth century. During this period when the Brookes of Summerton were experiencing financial bother of sorts, Baronet George Frederick commented 'one can hardly wonder at the state to which the gentry have been reduced, when the smell of roast beef can be detected emanating from the gate lodges.' Obviously well fed tenantry had a negative impact on the wealth of the gentry.

In *The Brimming River* Raymond F. Brooke tells of his schooldays in an English public school and his visits to Madam Tussaud's and the Aquarium. Among the attractions at the Aquarium was a circus of performing fleas. They pulled little cars and swung back and forth on tiny swings, and after the show the owner fed them from his own arm and placed them in cotton wool until their next performance.

Such was the popularity of this circus, it came to the notice of Windsor Castle and the circus was invited to perform in the presence of Queen Victoria. The fleas performed spectacularly and the elderly Queen Victoria was much amused. The owner of the circus was packing up to leave when, to his dismay, he discovered one flea was missing. He mentioned to the ladies-in-waiting that he was most distressed as it was his best flea.

The ladies-in-waiting told the queen and she was sympathetic to the man's plight. The ladies-in-waiting joined in the search, turning over cushions and searching through the garments of everyone in the room. It was eventually discovered on Queen Victoria and handed over to its owner. He examined the flea and proclaimed that it was very fine flea indeed, but unfortunately, not the one he had lost!

The Brooke family had a cousin, Charlie from Avondale, who visited occasionally to play cricket. He was, however, known to take the 'sulks' if the umpire's decision did not go his way – he was the famous Charles Stewart Parnell.

'Rush-hour Castleknock' circa 1900
The large building on the left was used as a forge and then became McKenna's public house
and later on Myos
Photograph courtesy of Fingal Co. Council

The Brooke family were renowned for having one of the leading kennels of harriers in the country, the family being much celebrated within the hunting fraternity.

Letitia Marion Hamilton (1876–1964), daughter of Louisa Brooke, was a distinguished artist. A pupil of William Orpen, her painting 'Snowfall in Co. Down' is on permanent exhibition in the Hugh Lane Gallery of Modern Art. The Brookes more local contribution to the arts is a magnificent Harry Clarke stained glass window to St Brigid's church in Castleknock which may be viewed to this day.

The Brooke family sold Summerton to Thomas Kennedy Laidlaw in 1911, whereupon he renamed, or should I say, respelled it, Somerton. The Laidlaws came from Scotland in 1906, residing first in Abbey Lodge, Carpenterstown, which they purchased from the Manley family, later acquiring Diswellstown House and finally Somerton for use as a stud farm. The Laidlaws were originally iron-founders but later on moved into banking and eventually the manufacture of cotton thread. Their company J. & P. Coates became known worldwide for the quality of their thread.

St Brigid's church, Castleknock, circa 1920s
The building on the right was the telephone exchange. The thatched cottage to the front of the
church survived until the 1950s
Courtesy of Fingal County Council

T.K. Laidlaw was appointed high sheriff in 1919 and was also a steward of the Irish Turf Club. He was the last person to be appointed to the privy council before Irish independence. The English Derby winner *Aboyeur* in 1913 was bred by T.K. Laidlaw. It was known as 'The Suffragette Derby' owing to Ms Emily Davison who ran in front of the king's horse *Anmer* causing mayhem, she died from her injuries ten days later. She was protesting for the campaign for equal voting rights for women. The favourite in the race, *Craganour*, was disqualified for bumping, so, *Aboyeur*, the 100/1 chance won the race. Two horses owned by T.K. Laidlaw – *Gregalack* and *Crakle* went on to win Grand Nationals, unfortunately after they passed out of his ownership.

T.K. Laidlaw was one of the founding trustees of the Irish Hospitals Trust, along with his neighbour, Lord Holmpatrick and others. He was also a benefactor to Sir Patrick Dun's Hospital.

Abbey Lodge was demolished in 1982 and the Cherry Lawn houses in Carpenterstown are built on the former site. Duncan Ferguson, one of the Laidlaw's horse trainers, also lived in Abbey Lodge, as did Dana Harrison some years later.

Somerton House and estate was purchased from the Laidlaws by the late Phil Monahan of Monarch Properties fame within the past twenty years.

Recently The Tower Hotel Group and Paul Monahan, son of the late Phil, joined forces to develop a new hotel and country club, including a superb golf course. The Castleknock Hotel and Country Club consists of a 144 bed luxury hotel including swimming pool and fitness centre and the adjoining Castleknock Golf Club which boasts a championship course with several delightful minature lakes.

Diswellstown House, the Kennan family home, had a well with petrifying qualities. If a stick was placed in it, the stick would appear to turn to stone; an equivalent accretion to that of limescale in a kettle. Thomas Kennan was captain of the Thirty-fourth Regiment of Foot. The family also owned Annfield and Ashtown Lodge and were associated with the firm Mono Pumps. The Kennans' ironmongery supplied most of the ironwork in the Phoenix Park – railings, gates and so on. A family called O'Keefe also lived here.

Joe Manley was a famous local rider and trainer. He had twenty-three winners in 1909 and won the Farmers' Race at Fairyhouse in April 1915. His father, Thomas Manley, was presented with a silver cup from Col Pope of the Dragoon Guards for his services to horse breeding in 1889. The Manley family were noted for their bloodstock and indeed supplied warhorses to the British army for many years. They entertained King Edward VII at their Castleknock property at Laurel Lodge and staged a horse race for his entertainment at an area called the Gallops. The Manleys later lived in Roselawn House, having sold the properties in Laurel Lodge and Carpenterstown.

The Bradys of Laurel Lodge had the adjoining farm, which is now the Laurel Lodge residential area. During the First World War the army horses were stabled here for rest and recuperation. There was a brickfield on this property, the local clay being particularly suitable for this purpose. The church of St Thomas the Apostle in Laurel Lodge has a fine stained window from the Harry Clarke studio. It was originally in the Dominican Convent in Dun Laoghaire, as was the wall sculpture in the Day Chapel. The latter was sculpted by the Pearse firm of monumental sculptors, of which Patrick and Willie, both of whom were executed in 1916, were family members.

There is a hedgerow running at the side of the community centre and across the road at the rear of the church. It marks the line of an old road that ran from College Gate across Laurel Lodge and Roselawn and down into Blanchardstown at the church. All that remains is the Church Avenue part; the remainder fell into disuse as the Royal Canal cut through it, and it was not bridged. This road is marked in the Rocque Map of 1760.

Back in Castleknock village, Myos pub is on the site of McKenna's old pub, which was originally a forge. Opposite St Brigid's church was Castleknock Post Office where Miss Mary Breen, the postmistress, served for a record 56 years. She died aged 97 years and only resigned the position in 1981 age 93. Miss Mary Breen recalled seeing Queen Victoria returning in her coach from a visit to Castleknock College in 1900, as is related in this book. Miss Breen's father was a staunch supporter of Parnell. His employers, Castleknock College, where he was a teacher, disapproved of his politics.

They parted company following his appearance at a Parnellite public meeting where he stood on the platform. He went on to teach in Mount St Joseph's Roscrea.

The Penny Bank founded in 1824 was close by. Out of this grew the merchant bank of Guinness and Mahon. The Guinness involvement was through the banking cousins of the brewing Guinnesses. Sir Hugh Mahon, the other partner in the enterprise, had lands where the present Georgian Village is sited.

The Railway Bar, beside Brady's, was used in a scene from the film *Young Cassidy* (1965), which was based on the life and times of Sean O'Casey. The church of St Brigid originally had a steeple. This was removed in 1957 because it became dangerous.

A previous steeple also disappeared due to 'a western blast', as the following lines penned by Dean Swift in 1710 show:

On the Little House by the Churchyard of Castleknock

Whoever pleaseth to inquire,
Why yonder steeple wants a spire,
The grey old fellow poet Joe
The philosophic cause will show.

Once upon a time a Western blast,
At least twelve inches overcast,
Reckoning roof, weathercock, and all,
Which came with a prodigious fall;
And tumbling topsyturvy round
Light with its bottom on the ground.
For by the laws of gravitation,
It fell into its proper station.

This is a little strutting pile,
You see just by the church yard stile;
The walls in tumbling gave a knock;
And thus the steeple got a shock.
From whence the neighbouring farmer calls
The steeple 'Knock'; the vicar 'Walls'.

The vicar once a week creeps in,
Sits with his knee up to his chin;

Here cons his notes, and takes a whet,
Till the small ragged flock is met.

A traveller, who by did pass,
Observed the roof behind the grass;
On tip-toe stood and reared his snout,
And saw the parson creeping out;
Was much surprised to see a crow
Venture to build a nest so low.

A school boy ran unto't and thought,
The crib was down, the blackbird caught.
A third who lost his way by night,
Was forced, for safety, to alight;
And stepping o'er the fabric roof
His horse has like to spoil his hoof.

Warburton took it in his noddle
This building was designed a model,
Or a pigeon-house, or oven,
To bake one loaf, and keep one dove in.

Then Mrs Johnson gave her verdict
And everyone was pleased, that heard it.
'All that you make this stir about,
Is but a still which wants a sprout'.
The Reverend Dr Raymond guessed,
More probably than all the rest;
He said, but that it wanted room,
It might have been a pigmy's tomb.

The Doctor's family came by,
And little Miss began to cry;
Give me that house in my own hand;
Then Madam bade the chariot stand,
Called to the clerk in manner mild,
'Pray, reach that thing here to the child
That thing, I mean, among the kale,
And here's to buy a pot of ale'.

The Clerk said to her in a heat,
'What! sell my master's country seat?
Where he comes every week from town;
He would not sell it for a crown'.
Poh! fellow keep not such a pother;

In half an hour thou'lt make another.
Says Nancy, 'I can make for Miss,
A finer house ten times than this,
The Dean will give me willow sticks,
And Joe my apron full of bricks'.

The Rev. Charles Proby, one of the vicars who served here, eloped in 1691 with the niece of Archbishop Marsh and married her in a tavern. At first, the elderly prelate was enraged and reduced him to a curate, but he later forgave them. He was the founder of Marsh's Library beside St Patrick's cathedral. It is said that the prelate's ghost has been seen in an eternal search for a will placed in one of his books. This will would have disinherited his niece if it had been found.

The first church was built in 1609 on the site of the monastery of St Brigid, which, as we have seen, was founded by the Benedictine monks of Little Malvern. The present building was erected between 1803 and 1810. The lands of Mt Hybla were used as a residence for the vicars of the parish for a time. The following is a list of the vicars who served the parish of Castleknock up until 1961:

1470 Rev. John Fyche
1474 Rev. Meagh
1499 Rev. Richard Travers
1540 Sir John Dongan
1615 Rev. John Rice
1617 Rev. Roger Good
1638 Rev. Richard Matherson
1661 Rev. Patrick Sheridan
1662 Rev. John Lukey
1665 Rev. Elias De Vassel De Regnac
1669 Rev. Henry Monypenny
1691 Rev. Charles Proby
1695 Rev. Philip Whittingham
1710 Rev. Thomas Walls (friend of Swift's Stella)
1745 Rev. John Towers
1752 Rev. Kene Percival
1764 Rev. Richard Godley
1767 Rev. John O'Connor
1809 Rev. George O'Connor (son of John, above)
1843 Rev. Samuel Hinds (later bishop of Norwich)
1848 Rev. Ralph Sadleir (related to Lord Ashtown)
1903 Rev. Charles W. O'Hara Mease
1922 Rev. Robert H. Bodel

1937 Rev. Leopold A.P.W. Hunter
1951 Rev. William W.L. Rooke
1961 Rev. Erberto M. Neill

The following parish priests served the parish of Blanchardstown up until 1968:

1769 Rev. Richard Talbot
1783 Rev. Christopher Wall
1802 Rev. Richard Benson
1802 Rev. James Boyse
1803 Rev. Miles McPharlan
1825 Rev. Joseph Joy McDean
1836 Rev. Michael Dungan
1868 Rev. Gregory Lynch
1884 Rev. Michael Patterson
1887 Rev. Michael Donovan
1897 Rev. Patrick J. Tynan
1903 Rev. Stephen Fennelly
1926 Rev. Charles O'Carroll
1933 Rev. Thomas Hill
1933 Rev. Michael Cogan
1946 Rev. Kevin R. Brady

St Brigid's church from a sketch by Rev. Dr Wynne in 1790
This church pre-dated the one built in 1803

1954 Rev. Charles F. Hurley
1956 Rev. Patrick Kearney
1968 Rev. Morgan Crowe

THE GUINNESS FAMILY

The Guinness family has a long connection with the area, and its members were generous benefactors to the parish. They were excellent landlords and employers and their names are held in high esteem amongst the local people. Arthur Guinness originally brewed his beer in Leixlip. He purchased St Jame's Gate Brewery from Mark Rainsford in 1759. The original business had its ups and downs, to the extent that Arthur had to raise an axe to defend his brewery against overzealous government officials. He did not brew the distinctive Guinness stout until some years after taking up brewing. Sir Benjamin Lee Guinness, first baronet, became sole proprietor of the company in 1855 and built an enormous export trade. Arthur Guinness & Sons became a limited company in 1886 with a capital of £6 million.

Stout is believed to have been an English invention and its lighter version, Porter, took its name from the Covent Garden Porters who enjoyed it as their favourite tipple. It is thought that someone brewing ale burnt the hops accidentally and used them. The distinctive bitter taste appealed. So, 'twas invented in England but perfected in Ireland!

'... AND I'LL TAKE THE LOW ROAD'

The lower road from Knockmaroon along the banks of Anna Liffey to Lucan was famed for strawberry cultivation. The south-facing slopes are ideally positioned for fruit-growing because they offer extra sunlight. This advantage was used from early times in Europe in the growing of grapes. Indeed it would be a worthwhile venture today to try to grow some grapes on these slopes, given the fact that the summers are warmer nowadays. A glass of Chateau Knock would be nice with dinner.

In summertime, the population of Dublin came out on Sundays by pony-

Strawberry Beds from Doyle's Anglers' Hotel now the Anglers' Rest
Courtesy of Fingal Co. Council

and-trap hackney or sidecar to sample the luscious strawberries and wash them down in the local hostelries, the Angler's Rest, Strawberry Hall and the Wrens Nest. The strawberries were unlike the regular-shaped deep-red fruit of today, which are bred for the eye. It was of no concern if these strawberries were paler than today's and not all regular in shape: the taste of these juicy, sweet berries was exquisite.

The Wren's Nest was frequented by Brendan Behan, who wrote an article about its proprietor Hughie Ennis. Hughie was a great character and lived to ninety years of age, dying in 1972. His answer to those seeking his toilet facilities was to fling open the back door with the rejoinder 'out you go and mind the nettles.' An American visitor requesting ice in her whiskey was met with a solemn-faced apology explaining that he only had ice in season.

A lady photographer (a rare phenomenon at the turn of the century) had her pitch at the top of Knockmaroon Hill, where the various conveyances stopped to allow merrymakers to record their day out for posterity. A day's outing like this was a honeymoon for many Dublin couples of those times.

Whether the combination of strawberries and Guinness' porter was reputed to have aphrodisiac virtues is not recorded. The various strawberry-sellers lined the route with their produce placed on cabbage leaves. When one purchased the fruits they were sold with the leaf – organic packaging!

Mrs Carroll, a local lady, wrote the following in 1885:

Mount Sackville Convent is at the head, where young ladies, they are bred,
And taught by nuns of every form, the duties women's life adorn.
Beside it Mr Guinness built a tower. It has a clock strikes every hour.
It can be heard from far and near and gives the working people cheer;
It lets them know the time to quit; they may go home and eat their bit.

Near to that is the Seat of Knowledge, at Castleknock's St Vincent's College,
Where the clergy train up youth, and teaches them the love of truth,
And every virtue they require, for the Lord detests a liar,
Even when the truth they tell you can't believe them very well.

All along sweet Anna River, where the playful fishes quiver,
And the anglers patient stand to try and hook them to the land,
Mrs Williams keeps the Strawberry Hall. Never pass without a call.
She is a cheerful kindly woman, and will be glad to see you coming.
Her place was lately renovated, and you will be highly accommodated.

Next at the woolly corner you may stand and take a view around the land,
Carroll's cottage it is there, with flowers around to make it fair.
He is a moulder by his trade, and can show you castings he has made,
It's at the end of Somerton Road that leads to Lady Brooke's abode.
You will see her gates of wide expansion leading to her most lovely mansion
Where a family of the rarest of noble son and daughters fairest –
A loving mother they surround, the greatest blessing to be found
And now lovely grandchildren quite a score, if I could name them many more.
And from the terrace wall can view all that pass the valley through.

Gibney owns the Anglers' Rest, next Mr Gibney at the hill,
You will never see him standing still, he is always making some improvement.
He gives employment to the poor he never sends them from his door.
Mr Ennis keeps the Wren's Nest, a little further than the rest
And has charming shady bowers, where you might spend some happy hours.
There's also some lovely hills, but sad to see are idle mills
Falling down behind the waters, and our willing sons and daughters,
To another country sped, for to try and earn their bread.

Indeed Carroll's cottage is still there, with a sample of moulding outside. The present-day Strawberry Beds is a delightful area if you don't look up at the toll bridge overhead. The pubs along the route still attract business from outside the area and retain a lot of their old-world charm. The waters of the Liffey are a boon for anglers and canoeists and indeed the first salmon of the season is often landed between here and Chapelizod. Until recently square-shaped boats with nets and shovels dredged the Liffey here for fine sand. There was also a ferry across to Palmerston operated by a Mr Tracey, who charged a penny for the crossing. The ferry was discontinued in the 1960s.

WAR IN EUROPE, WAR IN IRELAND, EASTER 1916 TILL THE AUTUMN OF 1923, A FAMILY MEMORY

As it was Easter time, Paddy, as a special treat, had been allowed stay in his grandparents small farmhouse in Dunsink. The small 'farm' was really a cottage dairy with a couple of cows, some poultry, and a vegetable garden. The piece of land came with Grandpa Hanlon's job as a herdsman for a local landowner.

Paddy's home was in Convent View Cottages on Ratoath Road, about 1.5 miles further south on the road to Dublin. The dietary fare at Convent View was often supplemented by the produce of Dunsink, indeed part of Paddy's daily chore before leaving for school was to collect the cans of milk provided by the Dunsink cows.

The fine spring morning of Wednesday, April 26 1916 found Paddy fishing for pinkeens in the Ballyboggan quarry at the corner of Ratoath Road and the King's Lane, which was on his route home, following his Easter break in Dunsink. Paddy cautiously circled the quarry, fishing rod in hand, looking for a suitable perch on which to sit, mindful of his safety, as he knew this quarry was bottomless. Two items need explanation – the fishing rod was in fact a sally rod with a piece of catgut and a rusty hook, and the bottomless quarry has been filled in for the past 40 odd years. He was distracted by the distant roll of thunder – peering up at the clear blue sky he discounted the possibility of imminent rain. For the rest of the morning Paddy heard those remote rumblings of thunder until boredom and the hungry belly of a twelve-year-old drove him homeward bound.

On arriving at the door of his cottage, he was greeted by his mother whose worried brow softened into a smile of welcome relief. 'Thank God you're home son,' she exclaimed. 'There's a rebellion in Dublin since Monday. We only heard about it early this morning. The army is shelling Sackville Street – it's a wonder you didn't hear the big guns.'

The 'thunder' Paddy was listening to up at the quarry was the gunboat *Helga* shelling Liberty Hall, and heavy field artillery directing its fire at the GPO and other rebel positions.

This area of North County Dublin was, at that time, sufficiently remote for word of the Rising not to have reached most people until Wednesday of Easter week. The only phones were in the houses of the 'quality' and were probably not functioning, and post was obviously suspended as was newspaper publication.

Barricades belonging to both rebels and military disrupted horse-drawn and vehicular traffic to such an extent that travel had effectively ceased during the hostilities. Paddy's mother referred to the rebellion as being 'in Dublin' – today we would refer to it as 'in town'. Up to the time of his passing in 1981 Paddy always went 'into Dublin' not 'into town' as would most older people in the locality – indicating their perceived remoteness from the city, then the second city in 'the Empire.'

Paddy was my Dad, Paddy Lacey, and he told me of his experience of 1916, when I was a young fellow nearly fifty years ago.

TEN INTERESTING FACTS ABOUT 1916

1. Of the seven signatories to the proclamation, Padraig Pearse had an English father. Thomas Clarke was born on the Isle of Wright of Irish parents. James Connolly was born in Edinburgh of Irish parents. Eamonn de Valera, a senior commandant, was born in New York to a Spanish (or Cuban) father. Constance Markievicz and Erskine Childers were born in London. Maud Gonne MacBride was born in Surrey and Liam Mellows

was born in Lancashire. Michael Mallin, Connolly's deputy and Connolly himself had both served in the British army. Tom Barry, who later led one of the most famous flying columns of the IRA during the War of Independence, was serving with the British forces in France during the 1916 Rising while Erskine Childers was serving with The Royal Flying Corps.

2. The Court Martial Proceedings following the Rising were presided over by Brigadier General Blackadder who was half French. He was later used to portray the jingoistic type of upper class officers that surfaced during the 1914–18 War by Rowan Atkinson as part of the comical Blackadder series. In reality he was a conscientious officer and spoke very highly of Padraig Pearse.

3. Lord Wimborne, the lord lieutenant during the Rising, was an uncle of Raymond F. Guest who became United States ambassador to Ireland from 1965 to 1968. This relationship was not proclaimed too loudly during the fiftieth anniversary celebration in 1966 when Ambassador Guest was representing the United States here.

4. Brigadier General Lowe who accepted the surrender from Patrick Pearse at the corner of Moore Street, had a son, John, serving under him who actually accepted Pearse's sword. He later left the army and became a minor Hollywood actor and was, for a time, married to famous actress Hedy Lamarr. Arthur Shields also became a well-known Hollywood actor, though not as well known as his brother William Shields (stage name Barry Fitzgerald). Arthur was a volunteer during the Rising and was interned. He played the part of Rev. Mr Playfair in *The Quiet Man*. Thomas Ashe, one of the most militarily successful rebel officers was great grand-uncle to the actor Gregory Peck.

5. Dublin Castle was to all intents and purposes undefended. There was an attack on the castle and, in the fracas, a policeman was shot. The volunteers did not realise the castle was so poorly prepared and did not press home the attack.

6. Among those interned were a Russian national and a policeman who had both joined in the fight on the Volunteers side.

7. Sinn Féin had absolutely no hand, act or part in the 1916 Rising despite it being labelled the Sinn Féin Rebellion by the *Irish Times*.

8. Col Sir Neville Francis Chamberlain, inspector general of the RIC from 1900 to 1916, did not pay enough heed to intelligence reports about an impending insurrection and left the British military and RIC totally unprepared for the Rising. He also invented the game of snooker.

9. It is believed that British Prime Minister Herbert Asquith expressly instructed General Maxwell to cease the executions before James Connolly was shot. Maxwell, using the latitude normally extended to a general officer in a war situation, ignored Asquith's instruction and went ahead with the execution.

10. Nevil Shute author of the novel *A Town Like Alice* and *On the Beach* acted as a stretcher-bearer during the Rising. His father, Arthur Hamilton Norway was secretary of the GPO.

LOCAL HEROES OF 1916

The following volunteers from the area were involved in the 1916 Rising: M. Cosgrove; Abbotstown, A. Dowling, Main Road, Castleknock; C. Duffy, River Road, Castleknock; E. Duffy, River Road, Castleknock; P. English, Dunsink Cottage, Castleknock; M. Fox, Brasscastle, Knockmaroon; M. McNulty, The Mill, Blanchardstown; P. McNulty, The Mill, Blanchardstown; J. Mooney, River Road, Castleknock, P. Mooney, River View, Castleknock, Thos. Carthy, Castleknock, Thos. Robinson, Park View, Castleknock; J. Conlon, River Road, Castleknock, R. O'Driscoll, Ashtown; T. Bennett, Castleknock.

The following soldiers serving in the British army from the area were involved in the suppression of the 1916 Rising: H. Byrne, Lucan, Royal Irish Fusiliers (wounded); M. Carr, Mulhuddart, Royal Irish Regiment (died); J. Keating, Mulhuddart, Royal Irish Regiment (wounded).

The above names were taken largely from the *Sinn Féin Rebellion Handbook* (*Irish Times*, 1917). It is a list of those interned following the Rising and may include those taken mistakenly and could exclude some who escaped notice.

The list of those serving in the British army only includes those wounded or killed in action and does not list the number of local participants on that side during hostilities.

It appears many of the volunteers from the immediate area were engaged in the Four Courts garrison. Local actions included an incident where the railway line was blown up in Blanchardstown. This action was intended to prevent two trains from ferrying men and artillery from Athlone barracks to Dublin. A cattle special arriving in front of the troop train was derailed, however.

An 18-pounder artillery piece from Athlone was unloaded at Blanchardstown and used against rebel barricades in Cabra and Phibsborough. Because of a failure by the volunteers to render the permanent way unusable elsewhere, the train was successfully diverted to King's Bridge – now Heuston Station. The railway bridge at the Cabra Road was barricaded and there was some desultory fighting there.

Volunteers from Dunboyne under Sean Boylan with Dan Hannigan's County Louth volunteers had occupied Tyrellstown House in Mulhuddart with a view to joining with the Ashbourne unit in sealing off the North of the County. However, the initial successes of the Ashbourne unit had not continued and at this stage the British military had the upper hand. Therefore, nothing came of this manoeuvre.

In his history of St Margaret's, St Canice's and Finglas, Peter Sexton tells us that Paddy English and his family worked on the Abbotstown estate of Lord Holmpatrick. Paddy English was in the GPO garrison and was one of those arrested. Following his arrest, his employer fired him, and had his mother evicted from the gardener's lodge. Paddy English later went on to become a founding father of Erin Isle's GAA Club in Finglas. It must be said that English's fate was an aberration, as by and large, the local landowners, although almost exclusively Unionist, did not exact revenge.

Like many old soldiers, the 1916 men were reticent in relating their past deeds. This also held true of those soldiers returning from the battlefields in France or Gallipoli. The slaughter and the appalling conditions that Irishmen fighting in the British army experienced were not things a human mind would voluntarily revisit. This selective amnesia that was experienced on all sides was possibly a psychological means of avoiding what is known today as Post Traumatic Stress. Historians and people working for the folklore commission during the early 1900s described this amnesia when interviewing survivors from the Irish potato famine.

Soldiers serving with the British army had the benefit of records written up, typed, filed and preserved by officials delegated to this task. Volunteer armies did not have the facilities, finance or the staff or storage for such records. That's why I advise people to collate as much information as they can from the older generation who lived in those times and write that information down. The writing down of information is crucial as passing stories down from memory alone can allow factual error.

FIRST WORLD WAR CASUALTIES

Many brave men fell in the green uniform of the Irish Volunteers but many brave men also fell in the khaki colour of the British army. Thousands of men from the National Volunteers answered Redmond's call and joined up to fight for king and country. Many of these men died in France and other fields of battle. The following are the casualties from the area that I am aware of:

Allen, Joseph F., Staff Sgt, Royal Engineers died in Turkey, 4 November 1916.
Bannon, Thomas, Pte, Northumberland Fusiliers died in France, 12 June 1916.
Brabazon, Frank, Pte, Royal Dublin Fusiliers died in France, 12 June 1916.
Brennan, Christopher, Pte, Irish Guards died in France, 1 February 1915.
Bowen-Colthurst, Robert McGregor, Capt., Leinster Regiment died in France,
		3 March 1915.
Brooke, George, Lieut, Irish Guards, died in France, 9 October 1914.
Brooke, Richard R. Maude, Capt., Oxon & Bucks., died in Mesopotamia, 31
		May 1915.
Brown, James, Pte, Royal Dublin Fusiliers died in France, 1 August 1918.

Campbell, Patrick, Gunner, Royal Enginners died in France, 10 November 1915.

Casey, James, Pte, Royal Irish Fusiliers died in France, 12 October 1916.

Casey, William, Sgt, Royal Irish Fusiliers died in France, 12 October 1916.

Connell, Edward, Pte, Royal Dublin Fusiliers died in France, 16 October 1916.

Farrell, Patrick, Pte, East Kent Regiment died in France, 3 May 1917.

Farrell, Benedict, Lance Cpl, Royal Irish Regiment died in France, 21 March 1918.

Gallagher, Patrick, Lance Cpl, Royal Engineers died in Gallipoli, 26 July 1916.

Goddard, George, Pte, Royal Irish Regiment died at sea, 20 November 1915.

Harper, George A., Capt., Royal West Surrey Regiment died in Belgium, 12 July 1917.

Hope, William E., Lieut, Irish Guards died in Belgium on 6 November 1914.

Hughes, James, Pte, Royal Dublin Fusiliers died in France, 7 August 1917.

Johnson, James C., Capt., Royal Irish Fusiliers died in Turkey, 9 August 1915.

Kavanagh, Thomas, Pte, Royal Dublin Fusiliers died in France, 28 April 1916.

McIntyre, Percy F., Gunner, Royal Garrison Artillery died in France, 10 September 1916.

McCauley, John, Pte, Royal Dublin Fusiliers died in France, 11 November 1918.

McDonnell, John, Pte, Royal Dublin Fusiliers died at sea, 10 October 1918.

Murray, Thomas, Pioneer, Royal Engineers died in France, 10 April 1918.

Plunkett, Bartle, Pte, Royal Dublin Fusiliers died P.O.W. Germany, 25 June 1915.

Proudfoot, Richard, Pte, Irish Guards died in France, 15 March 1917.

Shanley, Thomas, Pte, Royal Dublin Fusiliers died in France, 15 September 1916.

Smith, Peter, Pte, Royal Irish Regiment died in France, 21 March 1918.

Stout, Patrick, Pte, Royal Dublin Fusiliers died in France, 26 April 1915.

Sykes, James, Lance Cpl, Royal Dublin Fusiliers died in Gallipoli, 15 August 1915.

Vaughan, James, Gunner, Royal Garrison Artillery died in France, 21 July 1916.

Vigors, Arthur C., 2nd Lieut, Royal Dublin Fusiliers died in France, 9 October 1916.

Vincent, Thomas James, Able Seaman, Royal Navy died in Jutland, 31 May 1916.

Vincent, Thomas Lucas Scott, Pte, Royal Field Artillery died in Belgium, 17 March 1916.

The above list includes a number of young officers whose only link with the area would appear to be that they were attached to the staff at the vice regal lodge before the outbreak of hostilities. They reported back to their respective units on mobilisation. Following their death they were remembered in memorials in St Brigid's church. There may, therefore be a more tenuous link with the locality – family or sweethearts perhaps?

The names on this above list are taken from the Blanchardstown Chronicle 1992 *edited by Peter Sobolewski and Colin Langran.*

LIVING & SOCIAL CONDITIONS IN DUBLIN IN 1916

When we look at the events of Easter week 1916 it is best not to look at it, or indeed make judgement on it, using twenty-first century eyes or ideals. We must remember that the flags flying over all public buildings were Union Jacks and the uniform worn by servants of the state military or police carried a harp surmounted by a crown. The pillar-boxes were bright red as were the dress uniforms of the military

There was a huge gap between the wealthy and the poor, and an Easter egg treat for the poor was literally that – a fresh boiled egg. For the poor of Dublin, meat and fresh eggs, butter and fresh fruit and vegetables were a luxury. Strong tea with a drain of milk and a cut of bread smeared with dripping started the day. Lunch (dinner) was again bread and, if lucky, a piece of cheese. Dinner or tea was usually boiled potatoes maybe again, if fortunate, with a rasher or sausage.

Families were large and in the centre of the city occupied one or two room tenements with one outside toilet and one outside tap serving 10 or more families. In this area most people lived in cottages or mud walled cabins with maybe a dry toilet at the rear. Water had to be hauled from a local well. Bedding in both areas consisted of a bed, usually well covered with old coats, to insulate against the cold or a straw mattress in a corner.

Tuberculosis was endemic and there were thousands of deaths from this and other diseases like diphtheria, measles, whooping cough, and pneumonia. Earlier in the century, the dreaded cholera almost wiped out the population of Finglas.

In the city centre, employment was at best casual and, in some families, unemployment affected three or four generations. In the locality of Castleknock and Blanchardstown the large estates of the gentry and big farmers gave employment to local lads as farm labourers, gardeners and servants. Local girls usually entered service as domestics or shop assistants. There was also a little work in mills and small factories.

From the latter 1890s, an effort to defeat Home Rule with kindness had raised standards slightly. The Boer War and other military actions had been good for agriculture and also had given employment in the army and navy. When Queen Victoria visited in 1900, she received a fairly rapturous welcome with some notable exceptions. The Dubliners came out in their droves waving tiny little Union Jacks for which we have been excoriated by our country cousins who put the moniker 'Jackeens' on us ever since.

When the 1914 war came, Irish business and agriculture welcomed it as did the working classes and unemployed. It heralded a boom time for industry, increased agricultural demand and work for the unemployed in industry, farming or the Services.

Most of the soldiers joining up did not join for the Empire or for little Belgium or because of John Redmond's eloquence. They joined up to feed hungry families. Some younger single men probably joined up for the spirit of adventure.

When the Rebellion broke out that Eastertide there was much confusion. Pat was in the trenches with the Dublin Fusiliers in France. What would happen to Pat if the Rising helped bring about a German victory? What would happen if the badly needed army wages were not there to feed 'the childer?' It would be like the 1913 'lock-out' all over again – poverty, starvation and disease.

Many of the men who would later feature as fighters in the War of Independence were honing their military skills in France or other theatres of war. Some families had a son in the green uniform of the Volunteers participating in the Rising, while another in khaki faced the might of the German army in Flanders fields. The executions of the 1916 leaders, followed by the threat of conscription, would remove that confusion.

THE WAR OF INDEPENDENCE

The headquarters for the Blanchardstown IRA during the War of Independence was the Farnan family's farmhouse in Ballycoolin. It was a good-sized two-storey farmhouse with a large barn attached. The farm was occupied and worked by the Farnan family who were tenants of the Rafters, a family well known in the dairy business.

The Farnan's house was set back two fields – several hundred yards – from the road leading from Ballycoolin Cross to Dolly Heffernan's pub. It was, therefore, an ideal position for a guerilla army to hide out.

In the 1916 Rising the opposing side conducted set piece battles. In 1916 Thomas Ashe for instance attacked Ashbourne RIC barracks in a battle facing nearly sixty RIC men. The RIC had eight men killed and fifteen wounded and the IRA had three men killed and five wounded.

The War of Independence was a different war; brain became more important than brawn. The engagements were short and sharp. Extensive intelligence work was carried out before the selection of a target. Great planning went into withdrawing safely after the battle, thus preserving the lives, weapons and munitions necessary to carry on the fight. There were exceptions as

198 ⁓✕ A Candle in the Window

in Cork and Mayo and also the burning of the Custom House in Dublin.

Fighting in the War of Independence was not as much the IRA against the British military as it was the IRA against the RIC, albeit an RIC strengthened by the Black and Tans and Auxiliaries. The British were sensitive to world opinion. The spectacle of the mighty British Empire coming down on a small nation would not have been welcomed. The British prosecuted the war as a 'police operation.' However, the RIC were well trained in the use of firearms and were well equipped militarily. The nonsense that the Black and Tans were the 'sweepings of British gaols' can be largely dismissed. Many of the Black and Tans probably should have ended up in gaols but to say they came out of them is not true. Most of the Black and Tans were non-commissioned officers and men who had fought in the First World War and many were Irish born.

Auxiliaries were drawn from the commissioned officer class. These were battle hardened experienced professional soldiers who were allowed 'carte blanche' to carry out a campaign of terror against both the IRA and the local populace. The military, on the other hand, were subject to greater discipline and acted more in a support role.

Jimmy Farnan acted as quartermaster of the IRA unit and Paddy was a volunteer as was the youngest boy Mick. Other members of the unit were Paddy Mooney the OC, Joe Thewles, Tommy Murphy and Mary Lynch, all from Clonsilla. Mick Hughes from Castleknock, Sheila Murray from Lower Road and Paddy Radcliffe, also Andrew, Michael and Lena Dowling who lived on the Navan Road near the tennis club. Michael Flanagan, Agnes Doyle, Mary Farnan, Elizabeth Kelly.

Tommy Murphy a blacksmith from Clonsilla and a member of the local unit was to have refereed the Tipperary and Dublin match in Croke Park on Bloody Sunday. He had to cry off as the Blanchardstown unit was acting in a reserve capacity to the Active Service Unit deployed by Michael Collins that morning to wipe out the Cairo gang spy ring. According to some reports the man who replaced him was one of those shot dead – this is untrue. The referee on the day was Mick Sammon from Kildare and he was not among the casualties.

In July 1922 at the outbreak of the Civil War the Blanchardstown IRA took the anti treaty side and many of them defended the Four Courts garrison. Three of the Farnan brothers – Jimmy, Paddy and Mick – were among those who travelled in to the Four Courts. During the fighting Mick was captured and lodged in Mountjoy Gaol. In the meantime word was sent to the family that Paddy was badly injured and had been transferred to the Mater hospital. He died there shortly afterwards from his injuries. He sustained these injuries when an exploding shell dislodged a defensive position and he was buried under a massive weight of sandbags.

Jimmy was unable to attend his brother's funeral as he could be captured, and Mick was refused parole to attend the funeral even though Jim Farnan the father, offered himself as a hostage. Mick agreed to sign an affadavit promising to never take up arms against the Irish Free State on the understanding he would be released. When he discovered that his release would not take effect until after the funeral he withdrew his promise.

When the funeral cortege arrived at St Brigid's Church, Blanchardstown, the family, friends and neighbours had to use 'their weight' in persuading the clergy to accept the remains into the church. The clergy refused a funeral Mass and refused to attend the burial, in line with official church policy at that time. The Capuchins of Church Street did not let the family down and provided a priest for the burial ceremony. There was more tension when the funeral reached Kilbarrack cemetery, as there was the funeral of an Irish Free State soldier in progress. The priest calmed things down and conflict between mourners on opposing sides in this war between brothers was avoided.

The end of the Civil War came with Frank Aiken's 'dump arms' order. The army arrived at the Farnans and took away the arms. Meanwhile, the republicans, who had been excommunicated, were taken back into the arms of the church. They attended weekend retreats at Rathfarnham Castle to prepare for their acceptance back into their church.

Lily Thewles was another local person who featured prominently in the War of Independence. Lily was a niece of Commdt Michael Mallin of the Irish Citizen Army, Connolly's second in command. She was born in Chapelizod in

1897. She was a founder member of the Womens Prisoner's Defence League along with Maud Gonne MacBride and Charlotte Despard. She was attached to the 1st Battalion Dublin Brigade from 1917. Her brothers Christy and Joe were in the Four Courts Garrison in 1922. She was apprehended by Free State forces while trying to reach them and was imprisoned in Kilmainham and later the North Dublin Union. She died in Connolly hospital at the great age of ninety-eight in 1997.

When a state of civil unrest occurs there is always a section of the population who will see it as an opportunity for making money. One such 'opportunity' resulted in two deaths following a raid on Rathbornes Candle factory on 19 October 1923. Three men, alleged to be dispatch riders in the employ of the Irish Free State army, raided the factory in an attempt to seize the payroll. The management of Rathbornes had reduced the amount of cash being held on the premises because of the troubles so the raiders got a paltry £43.

Eileen Chambers (nee Kinsella) who worked there at the time was interviewed by Bernard Neary author of *The Candle Factory*, an excellent history of the famous firm. She described how Willie Coates and Charlie English pursued the raiders. Charlie English followed them on bicycle as far as Glass's Garage, and was able to indicate to the police that they had gone in the direction of Caeveen graveyard. The police came upon them in a field and while they were being placed in the police car one of them shot Thomas Fitzgerald, a police detective, dead. The robber who fired the fatal shot and another member of the gang ran away. In an exchange of fire the armed robber was shot dead and the other was captured.

They appeared before a military court and the man who remained in the police car was imprisoned while the other was sentenced to death. His name was William Downes and he was executed by hanging on November 29 1923. It was the first hanging in the Free State.

Towards the closing stages of the Civil War other opportunists emerged – those seeking to settle old scores or venting old hatreds.

Two properties suffered at the hands of arsonists. On February 1923 Capt. Delhurst's stud at Greenmount was attacked by a party of armed men who doused the house with petrol and set it on fire. Capt. Delhurst was not living on the property at the time. The steward, a Mr Gore and his wife and child, who were living in the house, were locked in a room while the house was set ablaze. Luckily they escaped uninjured by breaking a window and exiting through it. The raiders also set fire to an adjacent hayshed. By the time the fire brigade arrived the house was substantially damaged, however, the fire was brought under control and local people helped in saving some furniture.

In a separate incident on the same day William E.H. Steed's hayshed, attached to his Clonsilla House, was also set on fire presumably by the same people. Steed had previously been subjected to intimidation as a consequence of agrarian disputes thirty odd years previously. Locals suggested Delhurst and his manager, Mr Gore, had some difficulty with labour disputes. Neither Steed or Delhurst's conduct would have been deserving of such extremely violent retaliation.

Much of the destruction wrought on 'big houses' has been put down to sectarianism or racial hatred of the 'British'. While no doubt this was the reason for some of these burnings and the anti-British nature of some of these actions was a 'tit-for-tat' for Black and Tan reprisals. It is true that some of this destruction was a type of class warfare similar to what happened to the French nobility during the 1789 revolution or in Russia during the Bolsheveik revolution. There was, it is thought in many instances, the issue of revenge being visited on landlords and gentry, who had engaged in financial and sexual exploitation of their tenantry. Domestic servants in particular were often subjected to extreme sexual harassment by their employers and the adult children of those employers. This was not an Irish phenomenon, as any perusal of English literature will disclose. No similar social upheaval occurred in Britain and the tenantry, therefore, did not have the opportunity to engage in this form of retribution.

This does not suggest that Delhurst or Steed had any record of harassment or exploitation. Information relating to either party is at present very scant. The barony of Castleknock at the time had many landowners who were untouched by all these events and most enjoyed a harmonious relationship with their tenants and employees.

The Civil War left a legacy of bitterness and brother often did not speak to brother for years. It is generally acknowledged that the GAA did much to heal the divisions created by this terrible war. The sport reunited the two sides that once stood shoulder to shoulder in a common cause for the five years of struggle that commenced on Easter Monday 1916.

10

THE BARONY TODAY

Castleknock barony today comprises the following townlands: Abbotstown, Annfield, Ashtown, Astagob, Blanchardstown, Ballycoolin, Cabra, Cappagh (Keppok), Clonsilla, Carpenterstown, Castleknock, Chapelizod, Corduff, Deanstown, Diswellstown, Dunsink, Huntstown, Johnstown, Mitchelstown, Mulhuddart, Pelletstown, Porterstown, Scribblestown, Sheephill and Snugborough. Formerly there were townslands known as Fullams, Glebeland, Irishtown and Lakes but these latter names fell into disuse in the seventeenth century.

Most of these names derived from families who arrived during the Norman invasion. The families of Abbot, Blanchard, Carpenter, Keppok, Deuswell, Hunt, Mitchel and Pilate thus have their names inscribed forever on the area, while their descendants no longer have associations with it and are scattered far and wide throughout the world.

Names like Cabragh and Scribblestown ('Skreybyrstown'), which both describe bad land, would have not been accurate descriptions given our present knowledge of the soil quality there. As we have already noted, Corduff ('the black or dark hill'), Clonsilla ('the meadow of the sallies', or willows) and Coolmine ('the smooth hill back') are Irish-language place names and are therefore much older, and predating the Norman invasion. The name 'Astogob' could mean 'the house of the beaks or points' or' the mouth of the waterfall'. In some documents it is spelt 'Castagob' or 'Stagob'. If we look at the names in the locality we see that the native Irish often named the area by topographical description, e.g. Corduff – 'the black hill'. The Normans tended to impose their own names on the area e.g. Cardiff Bridge, from the family of Kerdiff. This was a means of strengthening their title to the land.

The barony and its environs have been home to Celts, Norse, Welsh, Normans, English and a scattering of other nationalities, which make up the gene pool of today's Irish. We are all part of our past and our origins could have been a Norman knight, a footpad, an attractive courtesan or a Celtic chieftain. What matters is that we are all survivors and the descendants of survivors. When we think of the lives lost in wars, famines, rebellions and old conflicts and of those who perished by plagues and diseases we realise that our existence is the result of a master lottery. Long may our luck continue.

Another aspect we must consider is the suburban invasion of the barony, with grass replaced by concrete and hedgerow by houses. We can still see the odd elusive rabbit or fox that reminds us of the once-rural character of the locality.

I will the leave the final words to Patty Madden of Carpenterstown, who grew up when the area was rural. She says 'It was grand to wake up in the morning listening to the birdsong and cattle lowing in the fields. It was lovely but it was lonely. Now I hear the voices of children playing and it's great. I wouldn't swap that'. The children Patty was listening to and their children's children will write of these times and the part we played in them when they come to write the story of greater Castleknock!

Northern Cross Motorway M50 at Blanchardstown roundabout
Courtesy of Fingal County Council

11

GENEALOGY & LOCAL HISTORY

Many people tracing their family roots find local history books invaluable in their research. Similary, local historians find genealogical information gathered by those engaged in researching family trees crucial to their work. Bearing this in mind, in this annex I will list property owners (in excess of 1 acre) in the Castleknock barony, circa late 1800s and early 1900s, and also a list of registered voters in the barony in mid-1800s:

Property Owners with Holdings in excess of 1 acre Barony of Castleknock 1870:
Lord Annally, Woodlands (Luttrellstown) Clonsilla – 2,139 acres.
(Luke White, ancestor to Lord Annally, changed name from Luttrellstown
   to Woodlands because of bad reputation of some of the Luttrell family. It
   never took, its still called Luttrellstown today).
Lord Ashtown, Woodlawn, County Galway – 50 acres. (This relates to land
   owned by him in Ashtown).
Sir John Arnott, 11–15, Henry Street – 21 acres. Relates mainly to land owned
   at Porterstown.
Michael Betagh, Lohunda Park, Clonsilla – 188 acres.
Patrick Bobbet, Hansfield, Clonsilla – 521 acres. (N.B. the townland Hansfield
   was later changed to Ongar).
William Bobbet of Crickstown, Ashbourne, Co. Meath – 132 acres.
The above inherited his father Patrick's lands at Hansfield. The Bobbets came
   originally from France. A French mariner called Bobbet settled in Ireland
   in the seventeenth century.
John Brennan, Allenswood, Clonsilla – 87 acres.
Capt. John Turner Brinkley, Knockmaroon, Castleknock – 354 acres.
George F. Brooke Summerton, Somerton, Castleknock – 33 acres (a southern
   branch of the Brookes that numbered Basil Brooke Lord Brookborough,

one time Stormont Premier and Field Marshal 1st Viscount Alan Brooke among its relatives also of interest politically, they were related to Charles Stewart Parnell).

Gilbert Burns, Knockmaroon, Chapelizod – 33 acres.

Maurice Butterly, Corduff, Blanchardstown – 114 acres.

Madam Calixte Pichet, Superioress, St Joseph's Convent, Mt. Sackville – 39 acres.

John Connor, Castleknock – 1 acre.

Baron de Roebeck, Gown Grange, Naas – 1,660 acres (this is his total holding in County Dublin which includes an unstated amount of land near Tyrellstown, Mulhuddart).

Thomas Dunne, Ballyboggan, Finglas – 28 acres (Ballyboggan borders the barony).

Alexander Ferrier, Bellvue Park, Castleknock – 23 acres.

Maurice Flanagan, Deer Park, Castleknock – 45 acres.

Jane Fox, Pelletstown, Cabra – 4 acres (possibly associated with John Fox original owner of Halfway House, Ashtown).

Michael Gaffney, Barberstown, Clonsilla – 146 acres.

Amelia, Anne, Anne S., and Thomas Keenan, Annefield, Clonsilla – each ¼ of 345 acres (Annefield was the birthplace of Dr John T. Troy, archbishop of Dublin).

Thomas Kennan, Astagob, Lucan – 38 acres. (Astagob is in the barony of Castleknock. Lucan is a postal address).

Michael Kennedy, Blackhorse Lane, Cabra – 9 acres.

Edward Cecil Guinness, Farmleigh, Castleknock – 71 acres (today owned by government for entertaining heads of state).

Ion Trant Hamilton, Abbotstown, Castleknock – 3,647 acres (includes lands at Connolly Hospital and proposed St Francis Hospice facility).

Richard W. Hartley, Beechpark, Clonsilla – 330 acres.

Mrs Catherine Hill, Oaklands, Castleknock – 51 acres.

George Hill, Clonsilla – 58 acres.

William Hogan, Corduff, Blanchardstown – 107 acres.

John Hunt, Castaheany, Clonsilla – 73 acres.

Alexander Kirkpatrick, Coolmine, Castleknock – 870 acres.

Miss Mary Lawler, Chapelizod – 10 acres.

Bridget Ledwidge, Mulhuddart – 22 acres.

Capt. James P. Murray, Ashtown Lodge, Ashtown – 14 acres.

John G. Rathborne, Dunsinea, Cabra – 30 acres.

Ninian McEntyre, Cloverhill, Blanchardstown – 72 acres.

Henry J. McFarlane, Huntstown, Mulhuddart – 466 acres.

Ross Maguire M.D., Castleknock – 21 acres.

Simon Mangan, Scribblestown House, Cabra – 137 acres.

Joseph Manley (a minor), Castleknock – 127 acres.

(Major parts of Laurel Lodge, Roselawn and Carpenterstown – housing estates today.)

Robert Neill, Glenmaroon, Chapelizod – 143 acres.

Frederick O'Callaghan, Clonsilla – 47 acres.

Anne Toole, Chapelizod – 4 acres.

Trustees of Cabra Convent, Cabra, – 46 acres.

Trustees of Mercers Charity Schools, Ashtown – 127 acres.

Trustees of Morgans Charity Schools, Ashtown – 550 acres.

(Part of the above lands are today owned by St Brigid's GAA Football and Hurling Club.)

James Warren, Astagob, Lucan – 27 acres.

(St Mochta's church, Porterstown, is built on part of this land.)

William Willan Kilmartin, Blanchardstown – 121 acres.

The foregoing is by no means a definitive list, some property owners lived outside the Castleknock barony and unless I have information (which I have in many cases), I cannot identify the land holding. Some areas within the barony may also have been subsumed into Dublin city.

LIST OF THE REGISTERED VOTERS OF THE BARONY OF CASTLEKNOCK, FROM FREEMAN JOURNAL 1836 approx. –1865

Some address listed are not in Castleknock barony, however, the vote was based on property holding. Where the address is outside the barony the vote is probably based on property owned within the barony. The document is difficult to read, therefore, a few names and locations cannot be deciphered.

CASTLEKNOCK

A
1. Allen, Richard, Pelletstown House
2. Alley, Peter, New Park, near the Ward Hill
3. Archbold, Richard, Lisburn-Street
4. Armstrong, John T. Old Dominick Street

B
5. Balfe, James, Porterstown
6. Balfe, Patrick, Buzzardstown
7. Bayley, John William, 24 up, Gloucester Street
8. Blackburne, Mark, Barn-Hill
9. Bland, Jas. Franklin, Derryquin, near Kenmare
10. Bond, John, Tolka
11. Borbridge, William, jun. Parnell-place
12. Borbridge, John William, Powerstown, Mulhuddart
13. Brady, Pery Geale, Leeson Street
14. Brinkley, Mathew, Parsonstown House Clane
15. Broadbent, Robert, Chapelizod
16. Brook, George Frederick, Gardiners Row)
17. Brook, Francis Richard, Gardiners Row)
18. Burns, Gilbert, Knockmaroon Lodge
19. Byrne, Michael, Cabragh
20. Byrne, Patrick, Cappagh

C
21. Caffry, James, Chapelizod
22. Cahill, James, Allenwood
23. Callaghan, Christopher, Dunsink
24. Carr, William, Mulhuddart
25. Carr, William, Blanchardstown

26. Cavanagh, Thomas, Cabragh
27. Cavanagh, Thomas, Damastown
28. Clarke, John Read, Phibblestown near Clonee
29. Clarke, John Castaheny
30. Clarke, Henry Barth, Beechmount, Clonsilla
31. Clarke, Benjamin, Barnhill
32. Clinch, Thomas, Coolmine
33. Coffey, Mark, Coolmine
34. Coffey, Patrick, Pass-if-you-can, Clonsilla
35. Connolly, Thomas, Upper Gardiner Street
36. Connor, John Sheepmore
37. Cooper, Robert, Hartstown
38. Cooper, Henry, Hartstown
39. Cooper, Henry, Oakpark, County Dublin
40. Corbally, Patrick, Rosemount, Finglas
41. Cotton, William, Humphreystown, Blessington
42. Courtenay, John, Cappoge
43. Crosthwaite, Thomas, Chapelizod
44. Crosthwaite, Leland, Chapelizod

D
45. Dalton, Michael, Huntstown
46. Dennis, John, Ballygall
47. De Montemercy, Henry F. Tolka House, Finglas
48. Dioney? Thomas, Little Ballygall
49 Dodd, James, Coultry
50. Dodd, Christopher, Cherryhound
51. Dogherty, John, Stang
52. Donegan, Patrick, Castleknock
53. Donagan, John Cabragh
54. Donovan, Robert, Courtduff
55. Donnelly, John, Blanchardstown
56. Donnelly, David, Snugbourough
57. Doolan, Patrick, Finglas East
58. No name
59. Doolan, William, Castleknock
60. Doran, Joseph Henry, St Andrew Street
61. Doyle, Patrick, Corduff
62. Draper, John, Lower Camden Street
63. Duckett, Jos. F., Duckett's Grove, Castledermot
64. Duffy, Joseph T., Finglas
65. Duncan, James, Finglas
66. Dungan, Rev., Michael, Blanchardstown
67. Dunne, John, Mulhudddart

E

68. Elliott, Gilbert, Castleknock

F

69. Fair, Capt. Thomas, Clonsilla
70. Farrell, Thomas, Stang
71. Fegan, James, Castleknock
72. Fegan, Michael, Casteknock
73. Ferrier, Alexander, Knockmaroon
74. Fitzsimons, Peter, Coolmine
75. Fitzsimons, Patrick, Dunsink
76. Fitzpatrick, Joseph, Chapelizod
77. Flanagan, Maurice, Dunsink
78. Fletcher, Edward, Kilshane
79. Flood, Patrick, Astagob
80. Flood, Michael, Astagob
81. Fench, Lieut.-Col., Richard, Coolmine, Clonsilla
82. Foley, William, Redmills, Castleknock
83. Forrester, Mayor Chas., River Road, Ashtown
84. Fox, James, Pelletstown

G

85. Gall, James, Jun., Damastown
86. Gandon, James, Upper Gloucester Street
87. Gardiner, Francis, Cabragh
88. Garnett, Samuel, Damastown
89. Garnett, Samuel, Summerseat, near Clonee
90. Garnett, Thomas, Summerseat, near Clonee
91. Garnett, Richard, Summerseat, near Clonee
92. Garnett, Samuel, Jun., Clonee
93. Gerrard, John, Dunsink
94. Gerrard, John, Bay, Nr. Finglas
95. Gilbert, Thomas, Corduff
96. Glorney, Benjamin, Knockmaroon
97. Goddin, George, Long Meadows
98. Goslin, Arthur, Newcommon-place, North Strand
99. Graham, William, Kildare Street
100. Graham, William, Yellow Walls
101. Greene, Timothy, Capel Street
102. Gregory, Dr, William, Tolka
103. Greham, Edward, Woodville
104. Greham, Philip, Sheepmore

H

105. Halpin, James, Blanchardstown

106, Hamilton, Henry, Thomas, Clane?, Co. Kildare
107. Hamilton, Hans Alexander, Lower Mount Street
108. Hamilton, James Hans, Abbotstown House
109. Hamilton, Sir William, Dunsink
110. Harding, Wm., H., Rosemount, Cardiff's Bridge
111. Harding, William, Huntstown
112. Harding, William, Castleknock
113. Harding, George, Huntsjtown
114. Harpur, Rev. Thomas, Newpark, Maryborough
115. Harris, Joshua, Cabragh
116. Hart, John, Mount Prospect, Tolka
117. Harty, William, Upper Gardiner Street
118. Heaviside, Jn., Burrowes, North Blanchardstown
119. Heffernan, Richard, Ward
120. Hill, George, Clonsilla Cottages
121. Hill, Col, Philip, Diswellstown
122. Hoey, James, Buzzardstown
123. Hegarty, John, Corduff
124. Hogan, John, Porterstown
125. Holmes, James, Scribblestown
126. Hunter, James, Prospect, Finglas Bridge
127. Hutchinson, Frederick, Johnstown

I
128. Iberry, George, Long Meadows
129. Kane, James, Cappoge
130. Kearnes, Christopher, Grange
131. Keating, Thomas, Coolmine
132. Keegan, James, Pelletstown
133. Kellaghan, Laurence, Cappoge
134. Kell, M. Cheal, Ballycollan
135. Kemlre?, Capt., Jos. Henry Vincent, Castleknock
136. Kennan, Thos., H.P. Annastatia Cottage, Dalkey
137. Kennedy, Charles, Capel Street
138. Kirkpatrick, George, Donacamper, Celbridge
139. Kirkpatrick, Alexander, Coolmine House
140. Kirkpatrick, Alexander, Jun., Coolmine
141. Kirkpatrick, George, Rochfield, Celbridge
142. Knaseboro?, James, Castleknock

L
143. Law, Robert, William, Mountjoy Squre
144. Lawler, William, Damestown
145. Lawlor, John, Chapelizod
146. Peard, Thomas, Blackhorse Lane

147. Lectin?, Philip, Coolmine
148. Lestrange, John, Corduff
149. Lloyd, Rev. M. Humphrey, Fitzwilliam Square
150. Lynch, Anthony John, Upper Gloucester Street

M
151. Mackey, William, Coolmine
152. Magrath, William, Blanchardstown
153. Magan, Richard, Jamestown
154. Manley, Patrick, Huntstown
155. Marsh, Sir Henry, Castleknock
156. Martin, John, Heathfield, Cappoge (Lands now Cappagh Hospital)
157. Matthews, Stephen, Castleknock
158. Maxwell, William, Cruise
159. McCann, John, Jamestown Great
160. McCann, Rev. John, Castleknock
161. McDonnell, Michael, Cappoge
162. McFarlane, Henry James, Huntstown
163. McFarlane, Francis, Huntstown
164. McGarry, Robert, Cappoge
165. McGarry, Henry, Long Meadows
166. McGuire, Ross, M.D., Castleknock
167. McGuinness, John, Gallanstown
168. McGustee, George Murray, Blessington Street
169. McIntosh, Michael, Blanchardstown
170. McKenna, Patrick, Spricklestown
171. McNally, James, Gallanstown
172. Miller, James, Hartstown
173. Monks, William, Coolmine
174. Mooney, Andrew, Blanchardstown
175. (No Name)
176. Mooney, Matthew, Cloghran
177. Moore, Martin, Castleknock
178. Morrison, Wm., Frederick Court (North Frederick Street)
179. Mossop, Stephen, Mary Street
180. Mossop, William, Lower Sackville Street
181. Mossop, George, Wellington, M. William Street
182. Murphy, Patrick, James Street
183. Murphy, Dudley Fletcher, Francis Street
184. Murphy, John, Sheepmore
185. Murphy, John, Corduff

N
186. Nesbitt, George William, Finglas, West
187. Neville, Rev. William Alexander, Ashtown

188. Newman, James, Springmount, Finglas
189. Nixon, Frederick Peter, York Terrace, Kingstown
190. Norton, John, Cappoge
191. Nolan, Thomas, Johnstown
192. Nugent, James, Parkgate Street

O

193. O'Brien, Edward, Cabra
194. O'Brien, Anthony, Mountjoy Square
195. Oldham, William, Shfield?
196. O'Neill, Hugh, Coolmine

P

197. Pemberton, Frederick, Clonsilla
198. Piggott, James, Castleknock
199. Pigott, Thomas James, Castleknock
200. Pomoret?, Henry, Ballyboggin South
201. Power, James, Carpenterstown
202. Power, Edward, Diswellstown

R

203. (No Name)
204. Rainsford, Richard, Woodlands
205. Rathbourne, Henry Bayley, Scribbblestown
206. Rathbourne, William
207. Rathbourne, William Humphrey
208. Reddington, Thos., Nicholas, Kilcrnan?, Co. Galway
209. Reid, Thomas, Cabra
210. Reilly, James, Blanchardstown
211. Reilly, Edward, Ballycoolan
212. Reilly, Niocholas, The Ward
213, Reilly, Thomas, Finglas East
214. Reynolds, Francis, Philipsburgh Avenue
215. Reynolds, Laurence, Porterstown
216. Rice, Mathew, Anglesey Street
217. Rorke, John, Upper Temple Street
218. Roycroft, Gilbert, Carplenterstown
219. Ryder, Richard, Cabragh

S

220. Sadlier, Rev. Francis, Castleknock
221. Sanders, Fras. Alex, Abbeybridge, Castleknock
222. Segrave, Patrick, Castleknock
223. Shew, Richard, Jamestown House, Finglas
224. Simpson, Richard, Dunsink

225. Singleton, Edward, Collon, County Louth
226. Smith, Marmduke, Finglas
227. Smith, Thomas, Corduff
228. Smith, John, Bailestown?
229. Smith, Thomas, Cappoge
230. Smyth, Anthony, Diswellstown
231. Smyth, John, Sheepmore
232. Stone, Rev. William, Carpenterstown
233. Sugden, Henry, Diswellstown
234. Sullivan, Thomas, Corduff

T
235. Tennant, Charles, Mespil Parade
236. Thompson, Rev. Sheffington, Broomfield, Lucan
237. Thompson, William, Hollywoodrath
238. Thompson, Thomas, Tyrrellstown House
239. Thornton, Patrick, Cappoge
240. Tolan, James, Cappoge
241. Toole, Mathew, Chapelizod
242. Trumlville?, Rob. Nathaniel, Beechwood, Malahide
243. Tuite, Patrick, Astagob
244. Tuite, William, Astagob
245. Tyrrell, James, Cardiff's Bridge

W
246. Walker, John, Chapelizod
247. Walmesley, Wm., Gerrard, Mount Sackville
248. Walsh, Rev. Robert, Finglas
249. Walsh, James, Barnhill
250. Watkins, William, Finglas West
251. Wharton, John Lee, York Street
252. White, Col Henry, Woodlands
253. Wilkinson, John, Powerstown
254. Wilan, Thomas, Hansfield
255. Wilan, Benjamin, Mitchelstown, Finglas
256. Wilan, William, Kilmartin
257. Wilson, Mark, Cottage, Up Grange Gorman
258. Wilson, John Rusk?, Co. Meath
259. Wolfe, Wm. Standish, Whitworth Place

Y
260. Yorrell, John, 20, Smithfield

SELECT BIBLIOGRAPHY

Arnold, L.J., *The Restoration Land Settlement in Co. Dublin*, Irish Academic Press, 1993.

Ball, F.E., *History of County Dublin*, Gill & Macmillan, 1906.

Bennett, Richard, *The Black and Tans*, Barnes & Noble, 1995.

Breen Dan, *My Fight for Irish Freedom*, Anvil Books, 1989.

Brook, Raymond F., *The Brimming River*, Allen Figgis, 1961.

Brookborough Papers Public Records Office Northern Ireland.

Burke's Peerage.

Byrne, Joseph, *Byrnes Dictionary of Irish Local History*, Mercier Press, 2004.

Church of Ireland, Short History, Church of Ireland publication.

Cafferky, John & Hannafin, Kevin, *Scandal & Betrayal, Shackleton & The Irish Crown Jewels*, The Collins Press, 2002.

Clarke, Peter, *The Royal Canal: The Complete Story*, Elo Publications, 1992.

Collins, M.E., *Conquest & Colonisation*, Gill & Macmillan, 1969.

Coots, R.J., *The Middle Ages*, Longman Group, 1972.

Cosgrave, Dillon, *North Dublin City & Environs*, Gill, 1909.

Coyne, Cecil, D*ublin 15 and Beyond*, Published by Blanchardstown & Tidy Town Committee.

Cullen, C., and Kelly, P.A., *A History of St Brigid's Church*, Blanchardstown, 1997.

Curran, Simon, *A Short History of Dunsinea House*, An Foras Taluntais, 1984.

D'Alton, John, *History of County Dublin*, Tower Books, 1976.

Dictionary of National Biography, Oxford University Press, 1937.

Farnan, J., *Notes on War of Independence & Civil War* (Unpublished family notes).

Finglas through the Ages, Finglas Environmental Heritage Project, 1991.

French, Noel E., T*he Battle of the Boyne, 1690*, Trymme Press, 1989.

Heerlihy, Jim, *The Royal Irish Constabulary*, Four Courts Press 1999.

Hickey, D.J., & Doherty, J.E., *A New Dictionary of Irish History from 1800*, Gill & Macmillan, 2005.

Jordan, Anthony J., *Churchill – A Founder of Modern Ireland*, Westport Books, 1995.

Joyce, P. Weston, *Irish Local Names Explained*, Fitzhouse Books, 1990.

Joyce, Weston St John, *The Neighbourhood of Dublin*, Hughes & Hughes, 1912.

Keegan, John, & Wheatcroft, Andrew, *Who's Who in Military History,* Hutchinson 1987.

Lewis' *Topographical Dictionary*, 1837.

Liddy, Pat, *History of Ongar*, Manor Park Homebuilders.

Mackey, Rex, *Windward of the Law,* Roundhall Press, 1992.

McC. Dix., E.R., *Irish Builder 1898: The Lesser Castles of Dublin.*

McLoughlin, E.P., *Castleknock Skeletal Material,* Stationery Office Dublin, 1950.

McMahon, Finn, *When Handball Made Headlines*, 1968.

McNally, Vincent J., *Reform, Revolution & Reaction*, University Press of America, 1930.

Meagher, Rev. John and M.G., *Historical Notes Caeveen and Early Parish, Graham Cumming,* The Church Publishers, 1954.

Moloney, Senan, *The Phoenix Park Murders*, Mercier Press 2006.

Mulvihill, Mary, *Ingenious Ireland*, Town House & Country House Ltd., 2002.

Musgrave, Bart., Sir Richard, *Musgrave's Irish Rebellion,* ed. J. Milliken, 1799.

Neary, Bernard, *A History of Cabra and Phibsboro,* Lenhar Community Press, 1984.

Neary, Bernard, *Dublin 7*, Lenhar Publications, 1992.

Neary, Bernard, *The Candle Factory,* The Lilliput Press, 1998.

Neeson, Eoin, *The Civil War 1922–23*, Poolbeg, 1989.

Nolan, Brendan, *Phoenix Park: A History and Guidebook*, The Liffey Press, 2006.

O'Beirne, J.W., *History of Phoenix Park*, 1930. (Publisher Unknown)

O'Driscoll, James, *Cnucha: A History of Castleknock,* 1977. (Published by author)

O'Reardon, Rev. W., *Historical Notes of St Brigid's Yearboo*k (St Brigids Parish, Blanchardstown)

Petty, Sir William, *The Down Survey*, 1655.

Reportorium Novum, Dublin Diocesan Historical Record, Veritas, 1971.

Roche, Richard, *The Norman Invasion of Ireland*, Anvil Books, 1995.

The Royal Canal, OPW Leaflet.

Rutty, John, *Natural History of Co. Dublin*, 1772.

Sexton, Peter, *A History of St Margaret's, St Canice's and Finglas* (Published by author, 2000).

Simms, J.G., *The Jacobite Parliament of 1689*, Dundalgan Press, 1966

Sobolewski, Peter & Langran, Colin, *Blanchardstown Chronicle*, 1992.

Sobolewski, Peter and MacPolin, Donal, *Blanchardstown, Castleknock and the Park*

Twixt Liffey and Tolka, Cottage Publications, 2001.

Somerville, Large, Peter, *Dublin the Fair City*, Sinclair Stevenson 1996.

Sweeney, Clair J., *The Rivers of Dublin*, Dublin Corporation, 1992.

Townshend, Charles, *Easter 1916 The Irish Rebellion*, Penguin Books 2006.

Viking Settlements in Medieval Dublin, Dept. of Environmental Studies, UCD, 1978.

Wall, Maureen, *The Penal Laws 1691–1700*, Dundalgan Press, 1976.

Wayman, Patrick A., *Dunsink Observatory*, Dublin Institute for Advanced Studies, 1979.

Wren, Jimmy, *The Villages of Dublin*, Tomar Publishing, 1988.

NEWSPAPERS AND PERIODICALS:

Dublin Historical Records, The Tolka (Dublin University Magazine), Evening Mail, Evening Telegraph, Freeman's Journal, Illustrated London News, Irish Times Newswest Yearbook, St Vincent's College Centenary Record 1835–1935, Thom's Directory, History Ireland.

PAPERS READ TO ROYAL SOCIETY OF ANTIQUARIES OF IRELAND:

'The Grant of Castleknock to Hugh Tyrell', Brooks, Eric St John, 1933.

'The Tyrells of Castleknock,' Brooks, Eric St John, 1946.

PAPERS READ TO OLD DUBLIN SOCIETY:

'An Outline for the Life of Warren of Corduff', Little, George A., 1968.

'Norbury, "The Hanging Judge",' Lysaight, Moira, 1975.

'Dr Carpenter,' MacGiolla Padraig, Brian, 1976.

'John Troy,' Purcell, Mary, 1976.

'J. Sheridan Le Fanu's Chapelizod & Dublin Connection', Brennan, Kevin, 1979.

Index